MW01103215

Navigating Neoliberalism

Gabrielle Slowey

Navigating Neoliberalism: Self-Determination and the Mikisew Cree First Nation

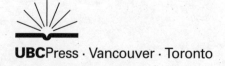

UBCPress · Vancouver · Toronto

© UBC Press 2008

All rights reserved. No part of this publication may be reproduced, stored in a retrieval system, or transmitted, in any form or by any means, without prior written permission of the publisher, or, in Canada, in the case of photocopying or other reprographic copying, a licence from Access Copyright (Canadian Copyright Licensing Agency), www.accesscopyright.ca.

17 16 15 14 13 12 11 10 09 08   5 4 3 2 1

Printed in Canada on ancient-forest-free paper (100% post-consumer recycled) that is processed chlorine- and acid-free, with vegetable-based inks.

Library and Archives Canada Cataloguing in Publication

Slowey, Gabrielle A. (Gabrielle Ann), 1971-
   Navigating neoliberalism : self-determination and the Mikisew Cree First Nation / Gabrielle Slowey.

Includes bibliographical references and index.
ISBN 978-0-7748-1405-8 (bound); 978-0-7748-1406-5 (pbk.)

   1. Native peoples – Canada – Economic conditions – Case studies. 2. Native peoples – Canada – Politics and government – Case studies. 3. Native peoples – Canada – Government relations – Case studies. 4. Mikisew Cree First Nation. I. Title.

E99.C88S54 2007   330.089'97071   C2007-903466-7

Canadä

UBC Press gratefully acknowledges the financial support for our publishing program of the Government of Canada through the Book Publishing Industry Development Program (BPIDP), and of the Canada Council for the Arts, and the British Columbia Arts Council.

This book has been published with the help of a grant from the Canadian Federation for the Humanities and Social Sciences, through the Aid to Scholarly Publications Programme, using funds provided by the Social Sciences and Humanities Research Council of Canada.

Printed and bound in Canada by Friesens
Set in Stone by Blakeley
Copy editor and indexer: Nancy Mucklow
Cartographer: Eric Leinberger
Proofreader: Sarah Wight

UBC Press
The University of British Columbia
2029 West Mall
Vancouver, BC V6T 1Z2
604-822-5959 / Fax 604-822-6083
www.ubcpress.ca

To the people of Fort Chipewyan

Contents

Figures

Maps

Tables

Acknowledgments

When I was headed into my fourth year of undergraduate study, I searched for an elective course that was outside the Department of Political Science. I was looking for something different to take in my final year, and my transcript was already saturated with political science courses. So I signed up for a course on Aboriginal politics offered at University College, University of Toronto, but the course was cancelled before it even began.

Disheartened, I approached the chair of the Department of Political Science, Robert Vipond, who informed me there was another fourth-year course on a similar topic, the politics of the Northwest Territories, that looked interesting and was undersubscribed. I immediately signed up, not at all prepared for the way in which it would change my life. The professor, Graham White, was a charismatic teacher with an enthusiasm for all things northern. I found his excitement for northern politics and indigenous issues contagious. And so began my journey into the realm of Aboriginal politics, arguably the most dynamic and interesting dimension of Canadian politics today.

After completing this course and securing my first A at the fourth-year level, I decided to pursue graduate studies at the University of New Brunswick, where I met my next mentor, Andrea Bear Nicholas, a Maliseet elder from Tobique reserve who was teaching at St. Thomas University. Taking her course "Natives and the Colonial Experience," I experienced a wonderful synergy among the students, most Aboriginal, but some, like myself, not. Her class provided a unique forum for discussion and opened my eyes to many of the issues, both theoretical and practical, confronting Aboriginal peoples today.

In the spring of 1997, immediately after completing my master's degree, I moved west to work for the Mikisew Cree First Nation in Fort Chipewyan, Alberta, through a program formerly titled Ooskipukwa, run by the First Nations Resource Council of Edmonton, Alberta. I would like to acknowledge the people of Fort Chipewyan in general and my friends from the Mikisew Cree First Nation in particular for their contributions to my career. I will never forget how they welcomed me into their community and into their lives.

Theirs is a friendship that endures, if not in regular communication, then in my fondest memories. They include former chief George Poitras, friend Denise Courtoreille (now Denise Kreuger), and Sally Whiteknife, along with her former partner Stan Wylie and their children, Nathan, Nicholas, and Shaleen. Matriarch Marge Glanfield and her husband, Oliver Glanfield, fed me quite often. Pat Flett and her family (Scott, Becky, and Thomas) and their extended family (Dana, Harold, and Hana and Sam) were also very good to me. The people in the band office, Bonnie Courtoreille, councillors Matthew Lepine and Steve Courtoreille, CEO Trish Mercredi, former CEO Lawrence Courtoreille, his brother Eddie, membership clerk Violet – almost everyone I met in Fort Chipewyan – were very kind and introduced me to the many dimensions of Aboriginal life and living. This is knowledge that is now part of who I am. In summary, these people did me the great honour of making me feel part of the community. They are the foundation upon which I have built my research. While I do not remain in touch with many of them, they are always close to my heart and in my mind.

Since completing this book, I have travelled in the bush with the James Bay Cree in Oujé-Bougoumou, around the world to visit the Ngai Tahu and Tainui of New Zealand, and across the country to investigate the workings of the Vuntut Gwitchin of Old Crow. Everywhere I go, I speak highly of my Mikisew experience. While some people I have met have accused me of being a cheerleader for this community, the reality is that when one is accepted or invited into a community as special as any of these, then one immediately recognizes the blessing of this experience. It is not so much about being a cheerleader as sensing the positive direction in which these communities are headed. After years of federal government intervention and mismanagement, this community is moving forward. While I am suspicious of government agendas and critical of the reasons for their support of self-determination, I also recognize the current reality of the lives of the First Nations people. Certainly, the absence of a real critique of neoliberal globalization occurring in relation to First Nations self-determination is problematic; but the world of First Nations and the politics that accompany them are constantly changing. These changes remind us of just how far First Nations have progressed in their struggle for self-determination, and they remind us of how far they have yet to go. What follows are my observations and analysis of the reality of Aboriginal self-government in Canada as it is unfolding.

This book was originally my doctoral dissertation, completed in 2003. I must therefore acknowledge the work of my examining committee: Gurston Dacks, Linda Trimble, Fred Judson, Julian Castro Rea, Frank Tough, and Frances Abele. I would like to extend a special thank you to my supervisors, Gurston Dacks and Linda Trimble, who read numerous drafts of chapters, offered insightful suggestions, and guided me throughout the course of this project. Their level of scholarship and patience is inspiring. My degree was accomplished with the financial support of the University of Alberta Walter H. Johns Scholarship, a SSHRC Doctoral Fellowship, the Federalism and Federations Doctoral Supplement, and the Northern Science Training Program Grant Award.

A thank you must be given to my dear friend Sara Maud Lydiatt, who edited the dissertation in its final stages and asked the important question, "Where is Fort Chipewyan, anyway?" Her question is the inspiration for the maps. Her time and support for this project are deeply appreciated and her contribution respectfully acknowledged. I also wish to thank the people at Syncrude and Suncor and in the federal and provincial government offices who participated in this project.

I decided to transform the thesis into a book in part based on the recommendation of the external examiner for my doctoral thesis, Frances Abele. This proved to be a fairly daunting task, eased in part by feedback from UBC reviewers and from my editor, Jean Wilson, but mainly through the strict review of the text by my friend, colleague, and former mentor/supervisor, Graham White. His time and expertise is greatly appreciated as the manuscript was significantly transformed as a result of his many suggestions.

Finally, I would like to acknowledge my family, which has supported and continues to support me throughout my constant travels in the name of research. To my parents, who babysat often and started me on this journey when they assured me I could do anything that I set my mind to. To my husband and my baby son, both of whom are very generous in allowing me time away to talk with many people and to conduct research that I find not only academically stimulating but also personally exciting.

Introduction

Over the past three decades, major changes have occurred in the relationship between the Canadian government and First Nations peoples in Canada.[1] Government policy on the administration of First Nations people, the settlement of land claims, and the negotiation of self-government have collectively changed the path toward Aboriginal self-determination. What has precipitated this change? Arguably, recent events, including court rulings, royal commissions, and First Nations political actions, have influenced the resolution of outstanding claims, the redirection in public policy, and the negotiation of self-government agreements. But none of these events has been a match for the state's need to provide for unimpeded exploitation of resources, especially in northern Canada.

Canada's relationship with First Nations is intimately tied to its ongoing search for resources. But although resource development explains *why* change is occurring, it does not adequately explain *how* change is occurring, nor does it sufficiently describe the developing character of self-determination. It also fails to address the extent to which self-determination is influenced by other important stimuli, such as globalization. Yet just as neoliberal globalization has changed "common sense notions" of the government-market-citizen relationship, so too has it changed the government-market-First Nation relationship.

What is neoliberal globalization? It is a decisive political strategy aimed at restructuring postwar capitalism in terms of its economic, social, and political dimensions (Hirsch 1997, 41). It is not only an economic force but also a political force that is inherently neoliberal in character. In the current phase of neoliberal capitalism, political actors have taken advantage of the restructuring of production, trade, and the interstate system by pressing for the decentralization, if not the dismantling, of national institutions (Albo and Jenson 1997, 218). The result is that neoliberal globalization has profoundly changed the welfare state. However, the "new political economy" (another term for globalization) has only altered the postwar social order, not eradicated it.

During the age of the welfare state, the purpose of state spending was to offset losses in private income during periods of heavy unemployment and to effect a more equitable redistribution of wealth among citizens. The Canadian welfare state therefore functioned as a mechanism to compensate for the discrepancies of capitalism and to reduce distributional conflicts among capital, labour, and regions. It also worked to balance out the fluctuations in the market. But if social spending and state intervention characterized the postwar political economy, fiscal restraint and laissez-faire economics characterize the new political economy.[2] This new emphasis is significant, because the elements of redistribution, representation, and equity that characterized the welfare state and that dominated the postwar era have been weakened in the new political economy by a regime that prioritizes privatization and market privilege.

The rise of these neoliberal forces has ushered in a new era of political interest in Aboriginal self-determination. While a shift in government policy is encouraging, neoliberal globalization is generally assumed to be a destructive force. That is, it could ultimately threaten the well-being of First Nations communities through its restructuring of market-state-First Nation relations and its reduction of the welfare state upon which so many First Nations peoples rely.[3] Indeed, most First Nations peoples already live as marginalized peoples. Because of the high number living in substandard housing, suffering high suicide rates, and enduring years of contaminated water supply, there is unease and a sense of foreboding surrounding neoliberal globalization. Indeed, concern is warranted and action is necessary. Yet, paradoxically, neoliberal globalization may be a reason for hope because of its emphasis on the independence of the citizen from the state. As such, neoliberal globalization may be a remedy to First Nations dispossession, marginalization, and desperation because it opens up space for First Nations self-determination.

What is it about neoliberal globalization that could lead to Aboriginal self-determination in Canada? Neoliberal globalization creates state governments with neoliberal priorities. Since states must revise their public policy to make themselves globally more competitive, neoliberal globalization therefore provides the rationale for neoliberal policies. Globalization and neoliberalism function as twin processes at both the ideological and empirical levels. Their overlapping influences are evident in patterns of change in the role of governments and in the nature of international economic activity (Klak 1998, 19). It is this overlap that leads to the misconception that state actions reflect global imperatives, when the opposite is often true.

Since neoliberalism favours a system of policies and processes designed to assist the marketplace, First Nations self-determination becomes more attractive than First Nations dependence on the state. As in other parts of the world, neoliberalism is reshaping the political and economic relationships of citizens and the state in Canada. Neoliberalism's ideal citizen is the individual who competes in the marketplace, is self-reliant, and does not act as a drain on the state. Thus, from a neoliberal perspective, the ideal First Nation is an independent First Nation that competes in the marketplace and is independent of the state. And from a Canadian neoliberal perspective, an ideal First Nation would be one that does not impede resource development activity.

Current Canadian support for First Nations self-determination reflects the historical and continuing need for the state to clear away political-legal obstacles for capitalist development of resources in Aboriginal-occupied regions. In general, neoliberal logic suggests that the well-being of First Nations in the new economic order is a function of their ability to compete as autonomous, self-governing, and self-sufficient entities in the global marketplace, rather than as wards of the state. Contemporary government policy toward First Nations thus focuses on (1) the settlement of land claims; (2) the transfer of programs from state to regional control; and (3) the renegotiation of the federal-First Nation governance and fiscal relationship.

An undeniable link exists between neoliberalism and contemporary forms of Canadian First Nations self-determination. Just as neoliberal globalization drives government policy, it also drives the construction of Aboriginal self-determination. This book examines the experience of one First Nations community – Mikisew Cree First Nation (MCFN) – during a critical period of transition (pre- and post-land claim). It highlights the parallels between the MCFN's self-government objectives, those of the primary industries in the northern Alberta region, and those of the federal and provincial governments. It also makes clear how First Nation self-determination, with its focus on increasing band responsibility for health, housing, and welfare, fits comfortably in the free market philosophy of a minimal state and non-government provision of services. That is, self-determination is consistent with normative and neoliberal goals of economic, political, and cultural self-reliance.

However, more is required than just a "good fit among [the] economic system, governing institutions and cultural standards" (Kalt and Cornell 1992, 43). Self-determination also requires direction and development by First Nations leaders and members who understand the linkages among social, economic, and political development and can invent their own solutions. For First Nations self-determination to be both sustainable and meaningful in the neoliberal age requires that political and economic control be vested in the hands of the people whose lives depend on it (Klak 1998, 257). It also requires a coherent vision, an economic strategy, and a capital base. With these ingredients, a neoliberalized form of self-determination can work to a community's advantage, as long as that advantage is measured in material terms – that is, advantage defined in terms of increased political authority and overall improved economic status.

A second important link between neoliberal globalization and First Nations self-determination is revealed in the efforts of First Nations leaders to take control of and make economic decisions on behalf of their membership. Since neoliberalism benefits those First Nations able to participate in a market society, those that do not possess the same economic potential or capacity must find a way to procure a capital base, develop an economic strategy, and address issues of economic development. Even without a large resource base, a community must still develop a strategy, one that concentrates on economic growth as much as on political jurisdiction. MCFN focused its economic strategies on achieving meaningful and equitable participation in the marketplace. Its goals of economic development and self-sufficiency have led to increased political autonomy and improved socioeconomic status. These goals have also led to increases in the community's economic activity through the development of successful businesses and joint ventures with international corporations, thereby enabling the community to contribute to and benefit from Canada's economic growth and prosperity.

MCFN may be the exception rather than the norm among First Nations communities (though my travels to date suggest it is in fact increasingly the norm). All the same, its story illustrates the importance of economic development for self-determination by demonstrating that economic development is essential to contemporary First Nations governance. It exposes the dual importance of political autonomy and capitalization. As well, it shows how self-determination functions as a vehicle for First Nations community-based development in the new political economy, moving the idea of self-government beyond the simple parameters of institutional arrangements to one of market-inspired governance.

Organization of the Book

The purpose of this book is twofold: first, academic, and second, practical. In general, research on First Nations people tends to focus on identifying the "Indian problem" (Wotherspoon and Satzewich 1993, i). In contrast, the present research does not seek to identify a "problem" per se. Instead, it traces the development of one First Nation's self-determination and connects periods of global political economy to phases in First Nations policy to demonstrate how state-market-MCFN relations have changed in the neoliberal era. More importantly, it seeks to highlight ways in which one First Nation (the Mikisew Cree First Nation) is navigating neoliberalism. While research generally does not affect living conditions for First Nations peoples, this book seeks to explain the struggles of other First Nations communities through this case study. While any effort to categorize First Nations is inevitably artificial, mapping self-determination is important, given its growing significance in Canada.

Although the conclusions drawn refer to the specific circumstances of one

First Nation, they are intended to provide guidance, wherever possible, to communities which may find themselves in similar circumstances, since "the sharing of resources and information may assist groups and communities to collaborate with each other" (Smith 1999, 105). Moreover, Smith suggests that the "spiritual, creative and political resources that indigenous peoples can draw on from each other provide alternatives for each other" (ibid.). Ultimately, sharing is beneficial, since the survival of one community can be celebrated by another. Hence, this book aims to share the experience of one community so that it may resonate in other parts of the country where opportunities exist to promote economic, social, and cultural sustainability through prudent and co-operative resource development. The challenge of sustainability is inseparable from the challenge of defining how First Nations construct self-determination and relate to resource development and different levels of government.

The complex dynamics of the globalization-First Nations relationship are best explored through the lens of a community engaged in the construction of their own version of self-determination. To sift through the intricacies of this inter-relationship, Chapter 1 explores the community dynamics of the Mikisew Cree First Nation (MCFN) at Fort Chipewyan. This chapter paints a picture of the community and the people. It explores the community's location, organization, and composition. It also describes the methodology used in the study upon which this book is based.

Chapter 2 discusses how, given all that self-determination entails, it requires a shifting of power, authority, and responsibility to indigenous levels of government. But political restructuring is only one component of self-determination. As former Assembly of First Nations chief Ovide Mercredi once argued, "If we gain [political] power for the community but we don't get the economy, we have power that cannot exercise itself" (Mercredi 1994, 7). Accordingly, for First Nations governments to function independently and for First Nations people to reduce their dependence on government, First Nations must similarly reduce their levels of economic dependence on the federal government. Self-determination, therefore, requires much more than transforming the current political condition of First Nations people.

Chapter 3 traces MCFN's quest for self-determination and the events which ultimately led to its political and economic transformation. This chapter explores the origins of the Crown-MCFN relationship, which arose out of global pressures for resources, mercantilist trade, and settlement. Chapters 4 and 5 investigate the more recent political economy of First Nations self-determination, in the age of neoliberalism, by exploring the transformative experiences of MCFN in political and economic dimensions. These chapters trace the neoliberal development of the MCFN-market-state relationship to reveal connections among market demands, state policy, and self-determination.

Chapter 6 concludes that transforming First Nations governance requires the reorganization of the First Nations economic relationship to the global economy. Self-determination is not only about reforming institutions or reconfiguring First Nation-state relation, but also about developing new relationships and creating new models of self-determination through market partnerships designed to improve socioeconomic conditions. Ultimately, self-determination is about moving forward. The conclusion also identifies ways in which the experiences of MCFN exemplify a growing trend among First Nations communities. These patterns can be useful for other First Nations in drawing comparisons to the MCFN experience.

Abbreviations

ABC	Aboriginal Business Canada
ABDI	Aboriginal Business Development Initiative
ACFN	Athabasca Chipewyan First Nation
CFA	Comprehensive Funding Agreement
C/FNFA	Canada/First Nation Funding Agreement
DIAND	Department of Indian Affairs and Northern Development
HBC	Hudson's Bay Company
IEA	Indian Education Authority
INAC	Indian and Northern Affairs Canada
KFN	K'atlodeeche First Nation
MCFN	Mikisew Cree First Nation
MESG	Mikisew Energy Services Group
MSB	Medical Services Branch
NLRHC	Northern Lights Regional Health Centre
NWC	North West Company
TLE	treaty land entitlement
WBNP	Wood Buffalo National Park

Navigating Neoliberalism

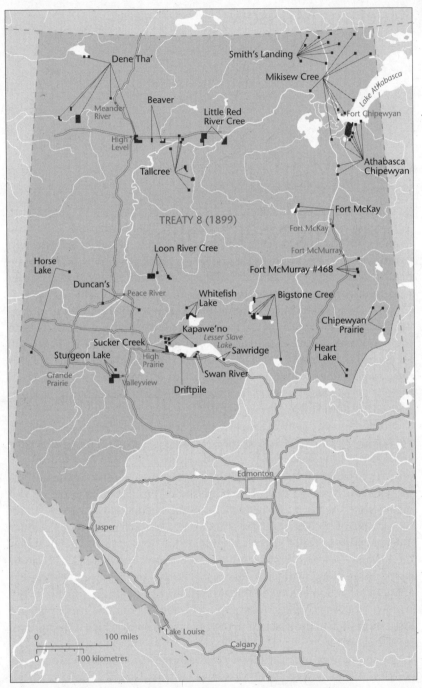

Map 1 First Nation groups in northern Alberta

1
Meeting Mikisew

This book tells the story of the Mikisew Cree First Nation (MCFN), Band Number 461, located in Fort Chipewyan, a remote village in northeastern Alberta, or – as the locals like to call it – "Fort Chip." Only accessible by plane most of the year, boat in the summer or, when weather permits, winter road from Fort Smith (to the north) or Fort McMurray (to the south), Fort Chipewyan is a picturesque community, nestled on the north shore of Lake Athabasca, in the muskeg of the Peace Athabasca Delta, immediately outside the boundaries of Wood Buffalo National Park (Maps 1 and 2). It sits 300 kilometres north of Fort McMurray, home of the world-famous oil sands. A river barge service is used to transport goods to the community, although there is no passenger service; and regular scheduled flights on Air Mikisew arrive daily from Fort McMurray.[1]

On landing at the Fort Chipewyan airstrip, one travels approximately ten kilometres of paved road to town, passing small lakes and an extensive amount of bush. Because it is a small community, life in Fort Chipewyan revolves around the post office and the "Northern," a remnant of the Hudson Bay Company general store, which are the two principal buildings on the main street. The town also boasts a beautiful wood lodge and hotel, which sits on a hill overlooking the lake and village. The town possesses a few other independently operated stores, a multiplex that houses a video-rental outlet, the Keyano College campus, and the Athabascan Chipewyan First Nation band offices, along with a few offices for MCFN. Also within the village are a municipal building, a Wood Buffalo National Park office, a provincial government building, a lumberyard, and a fish factory. From the centre of town, it is a short walk to the beach or to the Doghead reserve, which is the primary reserve of MCFN.

The community of Fort Chipewyan comprises three groups of Aboriginal peoples: the Woodland Cree (Mikisew Cree First Nation), the Denesolene (Athabasca Chipewyan First Nation, or ACFN), and the Métis (Fort Chipewyan Métis Local Number 124). Within the community of Fort Chipewyan, MCFN

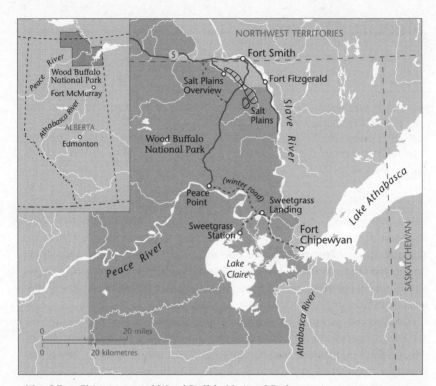

Map 2 Fort Chipewyan and Wood Buffalo National Park

is the dominant demographic group (Table 1). In 1999, the Fort Chipewyan population stood at approximately 1,400 people, consisting of 800 Cree, 250 Chipewyan, 180 Métis, and 170 non-Aboriginal citizens, among them RCMP officers, Parks, Fisheries, and Forestry staff, teachers, and nurses (Mikisew Cree First Nation 1999). Today, those numbers have shifted somewhat. The 2006 census reports a total registered population of 915 people residing in Fort Chipewyan of whom 822 are identified as Aboriginal peoples (Regional Municipality of Wood Buffalo 2006).[2]

MCFN remains the dominant group, however, with a total registered population of 2,408, of whom 773 are listed as living on-reserve (residing on one of the two residential reserves known as Doghead or Allison Bay) or within the hamlet of Fort Chipewyan, and a further 1,635 members living off-reserve, mostly in the cities of Fort McMurray, Edmonton, and Calgary. In contrast, the ACFN reported a total registered population of 834, of whom 239 live in Fort Chipewyan (DIAND 2007).

Unfortunately, there is a paucity of data on MCFN, which means there is no community information about gender, income, education, or employment. To a large extent, statistical data on MCFN are absent because prior to 1986, MCFN did not classify as a study group (since they did not live on reserved

Table 1

Mikisew Cree and Athabasca Chipewyan
First Nations registered populations, 2006

Residency	MCFN	ACFN
Registered members on MCFN reserves (or living in Fort Chipewyan)	773	239
Registered members off-reserve	1,635	595
Total registered population	2,408	834

Source: DIAND 2007.

lands). However, since 1986, no statistical data on this community have been collected or made available. In light of the lack of statistical information available at government (federal and provincial) levels, this study relies extensively on survey data retrieved from one of the few studies conducted, a community profile of Fort Chipewyan prepared for Suncor, a large oil sands producer in the region (deCardinale 1996).

I first travelled to Fort Chipewyan in the spring of 1997. Originally hired by the First Nations Resource Council (a program also known as "Ooskipukwa," which matches graduate students with First Nations communities in need of certain expertise), I acted as the self-government officer in the MCFN organization. My duties included reviewing self-government documents, liaising with government officials, filing First Nation by-laws, and preparing reports on government agreements. Working for the band, I integrated quickly into the community, taking part in the daily routines of local life, such as picnics at Dore (pronounced "Dorey") Lake and relaxing strolls out along the beach or to the reserve for ice cream, not to mention bush camping. I became very involved in community life and participated in special band events, including treaty days, a three-day event celebrating the past, present, and future of MCFN. There were hand games and traditional country food and, of course, dance competitions. Later that summer, I paddled down the Peace and Slave rivers in a canoeing event sponsored by Wood Buffalo National Park: a group of eight enthusiasts travelled three days in a voyageur canoe to Hay Camp at Fort Fitzgerald, on the Northwest Territories border. I also attended the Royal Canadian Mounted Police ball that was held in the community to celebrate 100 years of RCMP presence in the community.

Although my employment with MCFN finished in the fall of 1997, my connection to the community endured beyond this period. Over the past ten years, I have returned to the community on numerous occasions, as well as participated in other community-related events (e.g., personal meetings, regional conferences, and legal proceedings). My involvement in the community and my ongoing relationship with MCFN enabled me to earn a degree of trust. As a result, I was able to gather information through interviews and observations, as well as through the practical experience of community living.

Band Governance

MCFN is governed by a democratically elected chief and six councillors for a term of three years as provided under the election system of the Indian Act, specifically section 10, which provides for band elections based on the customary electoral system. As a band government, the chief and councillors provide Indian Act governance that includes the administration of membership, public finance, public works, economic development, social services, child care, and housing services. While some employment is available with the band, the Mikisew Cree family of companies is the largest source of employment for Mikisew members and others within the community of Fort Chipewyan.

MCFN receives approximately $25.7 million in funding from the federal government every five years. In addition to the federal government's fiscal contribution to its operations, programs, and services, MCFN has a net worth of over $35 million that is increasing at an average annual rate of 7 percent (deCardinale 1996, b-6). Collectively, its capital assets include businesses through which MCFN employs close to 200 local people, which translates into an annual impact on the community of roughly $5 million (ibid.). In addition, MCFN sits 300 kilometres north of Fort McMurray, home of the tar sands (known more commonly as the oil sands), a multi-billion-dollar resource extraction site that forms an integral part of Alberta's oil and gas industry and a source of economic benefits for MCFN.

Although MCFN appears to be a fairly cohesive community, income levels of individuals who live in Fort Chipewyan but work in the tar sands are substantially higher than those who remain in the community and depend on seasonal employment or government assistance. For example, income in Fort Chipewyan is influenced by the attraction of the "fly-in/fly-out" program. Sponsored by oil sands corporations such as Syncrude, this program ferries workers who wish to maintain a permanent residence in Fort Chipewyan back and forth to Fort McMurray. While recognizing the great expense associated with the program, the company feels that it is assisting the community by providing job opportunities locally, protecting the integrity of the community and Aboriginal culture, and effectively redistributing income. According to company officials, "We don't want to decimate the community. And we want those skills and that sort of affluence, if you will, to go back in to the community in terms of wages" (Interview with Syncrude representative 2000b). Yet the increase of material wealth is not shared equally, dividing band members even further apart by accentuating already acute levels of financial disparity.

Even though MCFN is not actually located on oil sands lands, the oil sands operations combined with federal funding provide MCFN a significant capital base from which to pursue and operate self-government. MCFN claims to be working toward self-government that would broaden its governance over all human and land services in the area. Self-government for MCFN means a stand-alone government with the powers to make laws, manage lands, and exercise jurisdictional authority, all under a constitution designed to guide its own activities. To facilitate the realization of its self-government ambitions, MCFN seeks increased autonomy and jurisdiction over reserve lands, traditional lands (primarily located in Wood Buffalo National Park), and commercial activities and properties in Fort Chipewyan. Their dream of self-government includes aspirations for increased powers similar to those of a province.

History of the Mikisew People

Fort Chipewyan was originally a fur trade post. The North West Company (NWC) built Fort Chipewyan in 1788 as an inland post for all fur trade activity in the area.[3] The Mikisew Cree, descendants of the Woodland Cree, migrated to this area to trap fur when the region was the focus of the trade economy. In 1821, Fort Chipewyan became the headquarters of the Hudson's Bay Company (newly merged with the NWC) for the entire Athabasca region. During this period, MCFN retained its bush culture, going to Fort Chipewyan only in the spring and fall for trade and provisions (guns, traps, and other manufactured necessities) or to attend religious ceremonies. Its economy thus combined subsistence activities and commercial trapping.

In 1899, when natural gas, oil, and gold were discovered in the Athabasca region, the federal government began to negotiate Treaty 8 with the First Nations people in the region. The treaty was significant because it established the foundation for the legal relationship between MCFN and the federal government. Comprising almost 325,000 square miles, the territory included under Treaty 8 was larger than the areas of previous treaties. It incorporated all the lands from Lesser Slave Lake in the south to Great Slave Lake in the north. It extended west to the Peace River country and east to Fond du Lac on Lake Athabasca. During the negotiations, MCFN Chief Marten worried about the loss of freedom to hunt and trap and about education for the children. He wanted to ensure that his people could remain self-supporting, in either traditional or alternative pursuits (Selin 1999, 13). In the end, Treaty 8 included annuities of $5 per person, medals and flags, health care and education provisions, and exemptions from all forms of taxation and military service. It recognized and affirmed MCFN freedoms to hunt and trap. Despite the formalization of the legal relationship, there was little interference by the federal government in the affairs of MCFN during the post-treaty years, thus enabling MCFN to retain its independence. This non-intervention was not surprising, given the laissez-faire ethos that dominated the period. However, in the era following the Second World War, when the federal government entered a new phase of interventionism, it began to build the social safety net on which MCFN members became increasingly dependent.

MCFN members lived in bush settlements well into the 1950s, at which time it became increasingly difficult to live off the land. With hunting and trapping resources dwindling and the fur trade declining, many began to move into the town of Fort Chipewyan, where there was a developing infrastructure and social assistance. In the ensuing phase of social and economic change, the Department of Indian Affairs and Northern Development (DIAND, with the Indian and Northern Affairs division also referred to as INAC) installed its own systems to support the changing economy and lifestyle in the region. During this time, the town of Fort Chipewyan essentially became a large reserve, as development typically associated with a reserve (i.e., health services, housing, educational institutions, band offices, water and sewage management, building of roads, etc.) took place within the settlement. However, the town was not a reserve, since no reserved lands had yet been set aside for or assigned to MCFN. Instead, Fort Chipewyan served as the centre of the MCFN community. Over time, RCMP barracks (1978) and roads (1978) were constructed, and a nursing station (1958) and water and sewage systems (1982) were built in and around the town site of Fort Chipewyan (deCardinale 1996, Chapter 1). For MCFN, this meant that infrastructure development did not occur on reserved lands but within the town itself.

The history of MCFN comprises a series of events that influenced, persuaded, or forced its development from the past into the present. The recent shift in the organization of the international political economy and development of the neoliberal state has greatly influenced and changed MCFN, in particular, over the past twenty-five years since the final negotiation and settlement of its outstanding Treaty Land Entitlement.

The Treaty Land Entitlement (TLE)

MCFN was a signatory to Treaty 8 in 1899 (see Map 3). A component of Treaty 8 was the promise that lands would be set aside for the exclusive use of MCFN (not to exceed one square mile for each family of five or 128 acres for each person). However, the government of Canada did not keep this promise and failed to provide any land in the years immediately following the signing of Treaty 8 (Fumoleau 1976, 72-73). During this period, failure to receive land was no serious consequence to MCFN, since MCFN did not want to be "parked on reserves."

In 1922, when the traditional economy and way of life began declining, MCFN asked for its reserve lands, but its request was denied. During the following sixty-four years, MCFN made forty more requests to Canada to "make good on its promise," but the treaty land entitlement remained outstanding (Selin 1999, 16). MCFN efforts were blocked, for instance, by federal

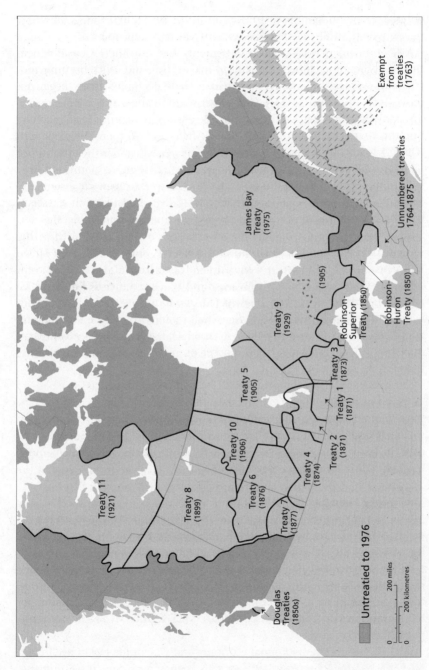

Map 3 Historical Indian treaties

Exempt from treaties (1763)

Unnumbered treaties 1764-1875

James Bay Treaty (1975)

Treaty 9 (1929)

(1905)

Robinson-Superior Treaty (1850)

Robinson-Huron Treaty (1850)

Treaty 5 (1905)

Treaty 3 (1873)

Treaty 1 (1871)

Treaty 2 (1871)

Treaty 10 (1906)

Treaty 4 (1874)

Treaty 11 (1921)

Treaty 8 (1899)

Treaty 6 (1876)

Treaty 7 (1877)

Douglas Treaties (1850s)

Untreatied to 1976

0   200 miles
0   200 kilometres

changes to the Indian Act in 1927 (repealed in 1951) that made it illegal for bands to raise funds for land claims without the permission of the Indian Affairs department. Eventually, the opportunity to negotiate a Treaty 8 land claim moved from dream to reality in the 1970s, when the federal government announced a new era of negotiation. At that time, in 1972, MCFN put forward its claim for a treaty land entitlement (TLE). The eventual resolution of the MCFN claim provided the catalyst for its political and economic transformation.

A TLE is a "process by which a First Nations group acquires the full amount of land to which it is entitled but never received as a result of signing a treaty" (Isaac 1999, 127). A TLE is a type of "specific claim" that results from an oversight or shortcoming by the government of Canada in the administration of land or the fulfillment of treaties.[4] These claims differ from "comprehensive claims," which occur in areas where no treaties existed previously. In the case of MCFN, its grievance fell into the TLE category. In 1986, after fifteen years of negotiations with the government of Canada and the province of Alberta, MCFN signed a TLE, a historic and transformative agreement. The TLE awarded MCFN 12,280 acres of land and $26.6 million. Alberta contributed the land and $17.6 million, while Canada contributed $9 million. Land allocation included nine reserve sites, including one in the west end of Fort Chipewyan, known as Doghead, one to the northeast, and one at Peace Point in Wood Buffalo National Park.

A Turning Point
The 1986 TLE represented a watershed in the evolution of self-determination for MCFN. It also connected MCFN to the new political economy. If globalization requires a stable investment environment to generate economic growth, then the resolution of land claims forms an important part of the neoliberal strategy. Settled land claims create an environment conducive to investment, required for all-important resource development, by clarifying issues of land title and resource ownership. Additionally, since neoliberalism favours the decentralization of programs and services, the TLE, by virtue of providing MCFN with a land base, facilitated government off-loading of control over band-related political and economic matters, proving once and for all that neoliberalism, government control, and resolved land claims are interconnected.

2
Neoliberalism Now

Because of the global intensification of capital accumulation, Canada, like many Western democracies, is currently shifting its state policies, form, and governing practices.[1] As the Canadian state strives to provide a favourable environment for economic growth and private enterprise, it is reconfiguring its relations with First Nations groups and their demands for self-determination.

Neoliberalism and Self-Determination
Self-determination is a multi-faceted phenomenon that involves the interaction of political *and* economic forces. It requires a First Nations community to control its own economy or, at the very least, delegate that authority (e.g., to a public government, as is the case in Nunavut). Self-determination includes the authority of Aboriginal people to govern their own people on their own land. Clearly, self-determination is a process that blends institutions (political and economic), which must work together to advance and improve the socioeconomic position of First Nations communities.

In its ideal form, self-determination does not simply refer to federal or provincial programs or efforts to normalize First Nations governments as junior governments in the existing federal system. Instead, it represents a First Nation's ability to govern in accordance with its own goals, values, and aspirations, which may or may not be neoliberal in orientation. Self-determination involves autonomy, accountability, and decision-making power. It requires significant amounts of political and economic control to make choices about institutions and economic activities, not only in a way that meets the needs, objectives, and goals of a band but also in a way that respects and maintains the culture and values of the community. It requires decisive control to redesign political institutions and fiscal arrangements. Finally, it necessitates the development of social, economic, cultural, and political institutions run by and for First Nations people.

Although the larger First Nations vision of self-determination is based on inherency, the pragmatic goal of self-determination is to achieve change within the current political and economic framework. In many cases, this goal requires negotiation of economic and political rights. Self-determination in the neoliberal context therefore refers specifically to First Nations political and economic development in the global economy and requires First Nations to be fiscally autonomous, since "without an economic base separate from federal and provincial funding, First Nations self-government would be vacuous; indeed, it would be a contradiction in terms" (Wotherspoon and Satzewich 1993, 244). Capital and an economic base are therefore vital for increased, meaningful political independence; and to that end, First Nations must strive to achieve some level of self-reliance and end their historical dependence on government. This requires the ability to make economic decisions that will ultimately enable them to become disentangled from the state.

In strategies for self-sufficiency, land is a central, if not fundamental, issue, because self-determination finds its most concrete expression in governance by a people over a defined population in a defined land area. Even though only half of Canada's First Nation population resides on reserved lands, "it is generally assumed by all parties involved, that territoriality – 'the actual or secured potential for control or jurisdiction over a defined land base' – is a precondition for First Nations self-determination" (Notzke 1994, 174).[2] If land is a precondition for self-determination, then the resolution of outstanding land claims forms an essential part of the process.

Land claims are not simply about grievance resolution or money. They are also about securing a voice in resource development. Connected to the struggle for land, therefore, is the struggle for access to and management of resources. Whether through the courts, on the land, or in the policy arena, First Nations have been actively seeking title to and participation in resource deals. The James Bay Cree, for example, won a 2002 deal to share resource revenue derived from new hydro projects, and the Aboriginal Pipeline Group in the Northwest Territories is a partner in construction of the Mackenzie Valley pipeline. Evidently, a common theme among First Nations is the need to benefit from resources on their lands.[3] Clearly, sharing the resources means more than splitting profits; it involves sharing the power to make decisions about the fate of the land and the resources its supports. First Nations control of, management of, and participation in resource development (though generally considered separate from, if not secondary to, matters of political and jurisdictional control) are thus becoming increasingly important.

The issue of land and resource-based self-sufficiency is controversial, since not everyone views First Nations territory or "reserves" as an appropriate basis for economic development and self-sufficiency or deems a reserve-based economy sufficient for economic development (Boldt 1993). Instead, many people believe that First Nations communities must develop off-reserve economies to survive. For this reason, many First Nations communities seek external investment opportunities. For them, self-sufficiency is linked to the development of partnerships, and First Nations communities are linked to the global economy. But partnerships might be difficult for anti-development communities such as the Deh Cho of the NWT. These communities believe that First Nations lands are being exploited by corporate profiteers who reap the benefits of resource development while First Nations people and the environment suffer. Procurement of land and resources thus provides the potential for First Nations participation in the global economy but also the potential for confrontation and exploitation. At the heart of the self-sufficiency issue is land and access to resources. Together, land and resources form the interlocking instruments of economic development and, by extension, self-determination. Though land and resources may have intrinsic economic value, they also have inherent political significance, for they provide the base from which First Nations can chart their own path and make their own choices.

There is no single model of First Nation self-determination. However, self-determination generally conjures ideas of indigenous governmental structures, rules, practices, and ideologies. The problem is that these ideas may not promote self-government but may instead promote a neoliberal form of self-determination. For instance, a First Nation may be self-governing, but its governance may reflect external compulsions (e.g., INAC rules, regulations, restrictions on the direction of policy, and even corporate directives). Self-determination means more than institutional arrangements. It means governance as the broadest possible system, one that includes state government but still permits First Nations people to make decisions. It is an inherent right that predates the foundation of the Canadian state; but it does not preclude a relationship with Canadian citizens and government, based on freedom, equality, and consent. It is a shared citizenship, one that does not require the sacrifice of those qualities that make First Nations people unique, nor does it deny them access to the benefits of modern society. Additionally, it acknowledges the desires and efforts of First Nations people to use their governments to achieve the goals they set for themselves, because self-determination provides them the opportunity to develop their own societies on their own land and for their own accord (Cassidy and Bish 1989, xix).

As neoliberal governments continue to encourage governance partnerships in which politicians and public servants share power with other sectors of society, the debate over "good governance" (such as that of First Nations self-determination) leads to important questions about difficult issues such as the role of government, the government's relationship to its citizens, relationships between levels and branches of government, and the suitability of different governance approaches to different stages of development. Non-governmental actors are critical in First Nations self-determination, but federal and provincial government involvement remains essential. This state-First Nations relationship is significant, because many First Nations people want to redefine their relationships with their national governments from a paternalistic and largely adversarial association to a more open, flexible partnership based on equality and trust. As practical matters of administration and service delivery in First Nations communities arise, issues of governance, partnerships, and processes arise that do not easily confine themselves to what a constitutional document says or what a government does. Rather, in many cases, self-determination requires First Nations to manage public society in a highly complex and interdependent world. The components, goals, and realities of self-determination are shaped by shifts in the international economy and rationalized by neoliberal logic.

Neoliberalism and Government Policy Change

There is great interest in the implications of the recent shift from the large, interventionist, and visible role that the state played in the postwar era to the decreasing, minimalist role it is playing at present. The renewed preference for the laissez-faire state, characterized by the absence of protectionism and state regulation, and the reluctance of the state to intervene in the market economy, has weakened the phenomenon of state intervention. As a consequence, rather than promoting national markets, "the federal government now pursues the elimination of borders between the Canadian economy and the rest of the world and works to make the country's competitive position in global markets the privileged barometer of well-being" (Albo and Jenson 1997, 215). The demands of external forces cause these shifts and shape Canada's internal development. As a result, the Canadian state has moved from assisting capitalism by providing for social needs to ushering in a new set of policies to promote unfettered markets.

The explicit transformation of state functions to meet the demands of a global market dominated by the United States has led to speculation that the sovereignty and the practical ability of the state to govern have been significantly diminished or, at the very least, transformed. Yet although the Canadian state's functions may have changed, the state itself is not disappearing. This distinction is critical, since government continues to be active in making decisions and policies that facilitate the accumulation of capital. This distinction also provides a useful analytical framework from which to understand changes in First Nations policy.

The unifying principle dictating current government policy, including First Nations policy, is that anything that increases corporate profit margins and enables them to produce efficiently ultimately serves the interests of Canada and all Canadians. Thus, government objectives have become largely identical to corporate interests (for example, resource development projects, lower corporate taxes, and so on). Today, as throughout Canadian history, there exists "an ideological hegemony emanating from both the bourgeoisie and the state which is awesome, which is reflected in the sheer pervasiveness of the view that the national interest and business interests are one and which certainly ensures the smooth functioning of the relationship between the state and the capitalist class" (Panitch 1977, 13). The Canadian state has historically served the interests of capitalism, in part, by dispossessing First Nations people of title to their lands which stood in the way of development. With the more recent development of neoliberal society, the state has changed its tactics, but not its goals.[4] Canada's new approach to First Nations policy is couched in promises of social cohesion and the prosperity of First Nations people, collectively and individually (Abele, Graham, and Maslove 1999, 251-52). Abele et al. caution, however, that the health and fairness of the relationship between First Nations people and Canada affects all Canadians. It is not simply a matter of getting along or accommodating each other; it is also a matter of reconciling outstanding conflicts between First Nations people and the state. This reconciliation is crucial because, "in public policy terms, the relationship between First Nations people and the government of Canada shapes the capacity of the federal government [and the provinces] to regulate land and resource use, to promote economic development, and also to address many other important economic issues that are critical to the position of Canada in the global marketplace" (ibid.). Although government capacity is not currently inhibited by First Nations claims, that could change; and largely to avoid those changes, the government has become involved in land claims. Therefore, the notion that the government is benevolent in its dealings with First Nations cannot be neatly separated from the economic imperatives also driving its policy.

Since 1969, when the government first suggested that it should release its tight grip on First Nations people by abandoning the Indian Act, Aboriginal-state relations have been undergoing considerable change (DIAND 1969). Over the past four decades, the state has concentrated on restructuring its relationship with First Nations people. This has occurred in an era during which First Nations people have asserted their political rights, claimed their land, and demanded a renegotiated relationship with the state. An essential part of this renegotiated relationship involves government meeting its outstanding obligations to First Nations people through the settlement of land claims. The decision to negotiate land claim settlements actually originates with the state; and as a policy initiative, the settlement of land claims is important to the state because it promotes stable economic growth. Land claim settlement is also necessary because of the post-*Calder* legal framework (see p. 33).[5] Ultimately, land claim settlement also protects the basis for material relations and Canadian wealth, since issues surrounding First Nations lands and resources have historically constituted an integral part of and a necessary condition for the development of the Canadian economy. This is why the government wants land claims resolved.

Resource development and exploration play a central role in analyzing the political economy of First Nations self-determination. As Clement and Williams (1997, 43) state, traditional Canadian political economy "cut its teeth" on the study of resource exploitation. The corpus of Innis' work in particular has come to be identified as the classic staples approach, and this approach is the logical point of departure for understanding Canada's resource development history. Staples are the foundation of Canada's trade economy, critical to its international position and to its First Nation-state relations.

In Canadian history, "two great staple trades have dominated the North, the fur trade and now, increasingly, minerals" (Watkins 1977, 86). Mining and petroleum industries share economic characteristics, since both involve highly capital-intensive exploitation of non-renewable resources (ibid.). As the gatekeepers to the land and its resources, First Nations people have played an important part in Canadian economic development. Already present upon the arrival of the first Europeans, First Nations people quickly became an integral part of the mercantile process as they participated in the production and exchange of resources and commodities. Yet that which made them valuable allies to the first traders also made them potential barriers to ensuing staples development. As the original occupants, they held underlying title to land and resources, a fact that was perceived as a potential impediment to the development of agriculture and non-renewable resources. As a result, First Nations people were disempowered, colonized, and transformed into wards of the state, primarily through federal legislation and related policies. This led to the pattern of dispossession, dependency, and devastation that has characterized more than a century of First Nations policy. As part of its approach to reversing this process – *decolonizing* First Nations – the federal government has embarked upon a new strategy to restore First Nations autonomy and authority as well as control over lands and resources.

Many changes over the last forty years in the First Nations policy field have been remarkable, for "First Nations people have moved from a position of political irrelevance to a position of considerable importance in the policy process" (Abele, Graham, and Maslove 1999, 252). This transformation has occurred because "we have moved from the concept of First Nations people as impoverished because of a paternalistic past [to recognition of] the need to resolve fundamental issues of land in order to achieve a more constructive future of [Aboriginal] self-control and improvement" (ibid., 284). While this is true, there is also significant pressure on the state to resolve outstanding conflicts and ensure stable access to resources, so that uncontested development may proceed, fulfilling demands in international markets.[6] Hence, the settlement of outstanding claims is as important to the continued economic growth of Canada as private property is to capital, especially since the colonial entity of contemporary Canada remains "firmly squatted on First Nations lands and cannot survive without them" (Green 1997, 60).

From the Inuit and Innu land claim that once threatened Inco nickel explorations at Voisey's Bay, Labrador, to the ongoing Deh Cho claim in the Northwest Territories (Park 2006), and the Mackenzie Valley pipeline deal in the Northwest Territories, unfinished business between government and First Nations groups seems to impede resource development. And as technology and market prices for resources make extraction more cost-effective, a large number of mineral and oil companies are particularly interested in developing resources in the North. Clearly, the settlement of claims is critical, since access to resources assumes access to land. Significantly, "land claims have already increased First Nations people's control over significant portions of Canada's land mass," and final land claim settlements have clarified questions of land ownership in many regions (Hill and Sloan 1996a, 48). This clarification encourages potential developers and fosters resource development. But the compulsion of the state to enter into modern-day treaties or to settle outstanding claims is not evenly experienced across the country. In a large number of cases (primarily across northern Canada), the political will to settle certain outstanding claims over others reflects an increase in the political and economic pressure placed on government by resource extraction companies.[7]

Pressure for Canadian resources is a prime force driving First Nations self-determination policy today, as are neoliberal policies (e.g., devolution, job training, and welfare reform) that promote market solutions to social and economic inequalities (e.g., poverty and employment).[8] As a capitalist nation with an economy – and particularly regional economies – still reliant on staple production, current policies and attitudes of the Canadian state reflect its support for the accumulation of capital and its penchant for market logic in the distribution of wealth. Historically, state intervention was an effective way to stabilize the dynamics of accumulation. Today, as multinational corporations seek an environment unencumbered by state regulation and social disruption, they benefit from an economic approach to governance in many regions of the world.

The Political Dimension of Self-Determination

If good government includes identifying goals and outcomes, then the neoliberal ideal of the common good rests on market-oriented values such as self-reliance, efficiency, and competition. The neoliberal ideal is for citizens to recognize their obligation to work longer and harder in order to become more self-reliant (Brodie 1995, 57). Applying this logic to First Nations policy, the neoliberal ideal for First Nations is self-determination, because self-determination re-establishes the proper balance between First Nations and the marketplace that was perverted by the welfare state, giving rise to an unhealthy dependency on the state. Hence, where the federal government once directly administered and governed First Nations, state-First Nation relations have shifted beyond supporting simple self-administration to the idea of degrees of First Nations governance. Similarly, federal policy that once aimed at assimilation is now directed at removing restrictions and developing First Nations economic independence and political freedom. Note that although the institutions of the state no longer perform all the roles previously associated with the welfare state, these roles have not disappeared or even diminished. Rather, other bodies or other levels of government, such as First Nations communities, have assumed responsibility for them.

The number of social programs that have been devolved to First Nations governments is growing, as is the power to make decisions pertaining to the delivery and management of programs. As many First Nations pressure government for more control over their affairs (through such measures as devolution and block funding), First Nations demands are becoming increasingly compatible with neoliberalism, as many First Nations seek to escape their status as wards of the state. As Nisga'a leader Joe Gosnell once said, "We're going to get away from being 'wards of the state.' Wards of the state, God it's insulting!" (Leake 1995). At the same time, it is also clear that this transfer of responsibility represents a fundamental change in the way that First Nations development policy is both perceived and delivered. In essence, state support for First Nations self-determination signifies a shift from making policy for First Nations people to letting First Nations people make their own policy, which is an important component of the neoliberal ideal of good government. One example is the 1985 amendment to the Indian Act, which for the first time gave First Nations membership powers to determine who was or was not a member of their community. Since that time, INAC has transferred control of education, law enforcement, commerce, health, and housing to many (but not all) First Nations communities. The result is that more and more First Nations have assumed responsibility for a compendium of social services and programs in their communities. The result is also an increase in the band's power, with elected band councils exercising significant powers, akin to those assigned to other levels of governments. This has the beneficial effect of transferring the responsibility for First Nations programming from the federal (and in some instances provincial) level to the First Nation level.

A cornerstone of self-determination is the ability to govern one's own programs and services. According to the Manitoba Public Inquiry, when "First Nations people seek the right to self-government they mean the right to determine how matters such as health care, education and child welfare are provided to their people, in their own communities" (Rozon 2001, 61). It is important that First Nations institutions take account of First Nations peoples and First Nations needs. For instance, new institutions "could mean creating a different kind of hospital, serving everyone but also responsive to the specific needs" of a First Nations clientele (Salter and Salter 1997, 329). Or it might mean "establishing a joint environmental resource board dealing with matters outside First Nations territory" (ibid.). It might even mean new arrangements for school boards, as well as First Nations schools. Finally, it could lead to innovative, collaborative arrangements for housing programs. So in addition to increased responsibility for social programming, devolution may lead to innovative service delivery arrangements and organizations. It may also lead to co-management arrangements with a variety of boards, councils, industries, and other legal institutions. The underlying objective, of course, is consistent with neoliberal objectives; namely, to transform every good citizen and every good First Nations person and community into a flexible, self-reliant body that makes fewer demands on the state.

The Economic Dimension of Self-Determination
The ideological shift associated with the advent of neoliberalism in Canada also tended to support the creation of market-based solutions in some traditional areas of social policy. For the First Nations economy, the result was a much stronger emphasis on the development of sustainable markets and businesses (Macdonald 2000, 171). But sustainable economic development requires access to capital, exposure to wider markets, development of labour-force skills, business-friendly communities, and stable investment environments.

Although neoliberalism requires the retreat of the state, within the realm of Aboriginal policy, the state remains very active in the development of new programs that provide Aboriginal people with the tools to participate in the global marketplace. For instance, the Aboriginal Business Development Initiative (ABDI) was launched in April 1999. ABDI was a $21 million business enhancement initiative designed to improve Aboriginal access to capital, to create an Aboriginal business services network, and to enhance the delivery of existing business support programs to Aboriginal entrepreneurs and organizations. According to the federal government, ABDI has been a very successful initiative, as recent years have seen tremendous growth in Aboriginal businesses: the growth rate of Aboriginal entrepreneurship is twice the Canadian average. In 2001, there were over 22,000 First Nations businesses operating across the country (DIAND 2002a). More than 30,000 First Nations university graduates provide the basis for a dynamic new business class.[9] Today, First Nations entrepreneurs are developing and bringing to market new products, services, and ideas.

Aboriginal Business Canada (ABC) is another attempt by the federal government to stimulate capitalist development in Aboriginal communities.[10] The ABC program supports technology use, Aboriginal youth entrepreneurship, and First Nations financial and business development organization. Since many First Nations lack the capital and the ability to exploit non-renewable

resources, First Nations enterprise tends not to assist the state in the accumulation of wealth.[11] The objective of ABC, therefore, is to forge a stronger
link between the Aboriginal business community and the broader Canadian
economy. As Macdonald (2000) explains, "the priorities of ABC are closely
related to elements of the government's overall economic strategy, particularly
support for a positive entrepreneurial climate, trade and market development
initiatives, a focus on youth, and the use of emerging technologies for growth
and productivity" (165). The First Nations business or the development corporation is thus a logical outcome of neoliberalism.

ABC represents one way in which government is working to promote
the development and eventual autonomy of First Nations business and
entrepreneurship. The orientation of ABC toward a form of government-to-
business programming also indicates a new type of governance relationship
between the federal government and First Nations communities. According
to Macdonald (2000), the "rich example set by ABC is couched in what can
only be described as an alternative governance model, particularly when
compared to previous initiatives for First Nations economic development"
(162). More specifically, it indicates a shift in economic policy orientation
from entitlements to partnerships. Macdonald suggests that "this new
governance model ... has supported the growth of so many First Nations
entrepreneurs over the past decade or so" (ibid.). This makes ABC a featured
program, given its function as the federal government's lead agency for the
promotion and support of First Nations entrepreneurs in Canada.

Federal programming for First Nations business development is critical
for neoliberal objectives. Federal support creates an environment conducive
to the reproduction of capital, thereby shifting First Nation dependence
from government to the marketplace. As former minister of Indian Affairs
and Northern Development Robert Nault explains, the department has
been restructured so that the government is now "working closely with
First Nations, First Nations business, the private sector in general, and of
course, the provincial governments, to talk less about jurisdiction and more
about practical ways of building a First Nations economy" (Barnsley 2001,
1). Because the government wants First Nations more involved with the
private sector and less dependent on INAC, it has also been building links
between industry and communities as part of this overall initiative. While
the modern role of INAC is largely that as a "hands-off" funding agent, it
also plays a "hands-on" advocacy role, most notably in promoting First
Nation labour and enterprise to the corporate community. It does this by
building First Nations economic capacity (e.g., through education and small
business initiatives), by encouraging First Nations to seek and take advantage
of market opportunities, and by working concertedly to promote a co-
operative relationship between industry and First Nations. In recent years,
interventions by the governments on behalf of First Nations have promoted

First Nation participation in resource development projects. According to one INAC official, "I guess from our perspective one would say it was a bit selfish – we wanted those communities to get the jobs and the contracts and the opportunities" (Interview with federal government representative 2000d).

Government encourages First Nations communities with land claims monies in hand to improve their social and economic status by participating in resource development projects. Furthermore, since land claims monies are often not sufficient to cover operating costs, government also encourages First Nations to seek out private sector solutions to funding, capacity, and program deficiencies. For instance, as First Nations engage in new social directions, such as welfare reform, their relationship with staples producers is critical to the resolution of welfare dependency. As one corporate official remarked, "The best social program is a good job" (Interview with Suncor representative 2000). The idea is that with a combination of corporate support and First Nations enterprise, First Nations can generate more jobs, which, in turn, means less unemployment and less welfare spending in the communities.

The neoliberal logic supporting the First Nation-corporate relationship is simple: "It is all about [how] a healthy economy is going to make a healthy society" (Interview with Syncrude representative 2000b). Many First Nations have expressed the belief that if only they had jobs, their problems would be solved. However, jobs alone will not eliminate the social problems that plague most First Nations communities. Instead, a combination of jobs, access to capital, institutional support, and community healing and training are necessary. Still, job creation remains an important step in the development of economic self-sufficiency for First Nations in the new political economy. With First Nations people now projected to comprise half of the workforce in the province of Saskatchewan within the next few decades (and Manitoba is not far behind), the First Nations labour force potential draws a lot of attention from government and industry alike. In addition to business development programs, human resource development projects and training programs assist First Nations people in gaining employment. Overall, First Nations need to develop comprehensive business plans, manage existing funds, develop management and infrastructure capacity, and partner with the private sector.

To draw on just one example from many, the K'atlodeeche First Nation (KFN) in the southern Northwest Territories received $441,000 in 2001 through the Indian and Northern Affairs Canada Regional Partnerships Fund to build new and renovate existing infrastructures of the KFN Industrial Park in Hay River (CBC 2001). Improving infrastructure is critical for northern communities seeking to diversify their economies, meet the demands of a booming economy, and improve the quality of life for their citizens. According to KFN

Chief Pat Martel, the federal government agreed to fund this venture because it promised to "create local jobs and provide new economic development opportunities for the region in the oil and gas industry" (DIAND 2002b). Federal support for this project clearly demonstrated the government's willingness to invest in infrastructure that facilitates First Nations market participation and development of the resource sector.

But to what extent does the resource industry provide a wage economy to northern Aboriginal people? There are no guarantees that employment in industry (such as the petroleum industry) will be secure over the long term – whether for First Nations or for provincial economies largely dependent on natural resource exploitation:

> Just as the fur trade's viability depended upon the availability of furs and a high world market price for them, so does the viability of petroleum development depend upon the availability of oil and a high world market for it. But what happens, for example, when the resource gives out, or if we in the south find a cheaper [or more environmentally sound] source of fuel in the next decade or so? What happens if the world market price of petroleum products declines to a point where it is uneconomic to exploit and transmit northern oil and gas to southern markets? The answer is obvious. The petroleum corporations, just like the fur traders before them, will pull out. But what will happen to the native northerners when this does occur? (Asch 1977, 59)

Asch raises important concerns about resource development and First Nations economic opportunities. But in modern self-determination, if the economy is unstable (whether modern or traditional, given the historical fluctuation in fur prices), First Nations have more ability than ever before to decide how to respond to uncertainties. Moreover, as communities seek to alleviate the potential increase in dependence on resource extraction, many use the *bottom-up* approach, making the economic engine community driven instead of state driven or industry driven. Diversification is an integral component of this approach, which means taking advantage of economic opportunities associated with local resource development. The economic challenge remains to find profitable market niches that are not already filled or dominated.

The contradiction for many First Nations people is that while the status quo of dependency and underdevelopment is no longer acceptable, a future characterized by increased resource extraction may also be unacceptable (Slowey 2001, 276). Many communities are internally divided over strategies of economic development. Within these community debates, voices arguing that land is a resource to be exploited for economic progress have become stronger. For many, including a growing First Nations business elite, self-determination succeeds only if it prepares a community to be self-sufficient and competitive in the global economy. In this regard, self-determination must seek not only to meet immediate, regionally specific needs but also to contribute to a wider vision of growth and well-being. A tenable vision for growth must strengthen the community's position within the global economy through participation in that economy. For many First Nations, this begins at the local level, since international resource development companies operate in their backyards.

Conclusion

Challenging the central argument of this book, which states that development strategies and neoliberal imperatives drive First Nations policy, is the assumption that the initiatives of First Nations people and their governments alone drive change and growth in self-determination policy (Cassidy 1990, 74; Anderson 1997, 1483). This assumption maintains that indigenous nations in Canada now exist within a climate of rapid social change and restructuring, and as dynamic societies, they seek to protect their future and their way of life (Abele 1997, 124). Absent in these analyses of First Nations self-determination, however, are theoretical considerations: structural and social explanations of First Nations self-determination as it exists under capitalism, driven by ideology and rooted in material relations. It is therefore essential to assess the extent to which the business agenda is central to international and domestic policy, Aboriginal policy, and self-determination.

First Nations self-determination may be an effective tool for meeting the needs of the new political economy, but is it also effective in meeting the needs of a First Nations community? Just as colonialism and capitalism are often treated as uniformly destructive to First Nations systems, globalization is also considered detrimental to First Nations self-determination. But just as First Nations are not monolithic or unified in organization, neither are their perspectives on or experiences of globalization. For some, globalization may positively influence their quest for self-determination. For others, it may influence their goals negatively. And for others still, it may be any combination of both.

3
Searching for Self-Determination

First Nation-state relations have historically been shaped by economic shifts that legitimize national ideologies and configure state-citizen relations. Just as MCFN political and economic development has been shaped by global economic demands and Canada's national development strategies, MCFN's quest for self-determination has been shaped by neoliberalism. Clear in this is that the Crown-MCFN relationship has changed since the relationship formally began in 1899 with Treaty 8.

Laissez-Faire Economics, Colonialism, and the State

Globalization is a relatively recent term used to describe an age-old process, one firmly rooted in colonialism. One of Britain's most famous imperial spokesmen, Cecil Rhodes, summarized the case for colonialism succinctly in the late nineteenth century: "We must find new lands from which we can easily obtain raw materials and at the same time exploit the cheap slave labour that is available from the natives of the colonies. The colonies will also provide a dumping ground for the surplus goods produced in our factories" (Ellwood 2001, 13). As global trade expanded rapidly during the colonial period, European powers extracted raw materials from their new dominions: fur, timber, and fish from Canada; slaves and gold from Africa; sugar, rum, and fruits from the Caribbean; coffee, sugar, meat, gold, and silver from Latin America; and opium, tea, and spices from Asia (ibid., 14).

The dominant ethos of laissez-faire capitalism and colonialism was predicated on a distrust of and hostility toward government intervention in the operation of the marketplace. Because of the laissez-faire philosophy, which accurately describes the economic, social, and administrative ideas specific to this historical era, the "magic of the marketplace" was left unencumbered. More specifically, laissez-faire capitalism, or classic liberalism, held that the common good was best served by the uninhibited pursuit of self-interest. It was that very doctrine of anti-interventionism which dominated nineteenth-century social and economic policy.

Laissez-Faire Economics and the Crown-MCFN Relationship
In the early post-Confederation years of 1867-85, the Canadian government, itself a colonial creation, was largely non-interventionist, participating only selectively in the development of the new country. Its participation was largely limited to the First National Policy (FNP), a series of policies that functioned as an important national development strategy, based on the premise of a new transcontinental economy that would unite the former colonies in the union. The Canadian government began to build a transcontinental railway, critical to the future economic growth of the nation (Brodie 1997b, 249). The FNP was formulated in response to internal political pressure and to the demands of a changing international political economy. The Canadian state transformed the West into a "frontier for central investment, a market for eastern manufacturers, and a source of supply for commodity traders"; and it moved quickly to foster and establish the new east-west economy, conducive to private enterprise and international competition (ibid., 250).

To build the railway and make way for westward settlement, the FNP strategy required the removal of First Nations people from their lands through treaty making. This strategy originally ignored regions of the North, such that in the early post-Confederation period (1870-88), the Canadian government had no interest in the Athabasca Delta region or the indigenous peoples who lived in the area. For the most part, the national government remained uninterested in the North, as it refused "repeatedly to acknowledge any responsibility for the Indians inhabiting the desolate country" (Fumoleau 1976, 41). As such, the government was simply unwilling to enter into treaty unless absolutely necessary. Even though some First Nations leaders in Fort Chipewyan expressed interest in a treaty to secure government assistance, the government maintained a policy of "no treaty, no help" during this period.

The Interventionist Interlude
After Confederation, the Canadian government pursued a policy of recognizing First Nation land claims only when the lands they occupied were required for settlement or development. The Athabasca region in Canada's northwestern interior was no exception. For more than two centuries, British and Canadian parties had explored the region and carefully inventoried its natural resources. In his travels down the Athabasca in the 1770s, explorer Peter Pond stumbled on "one of the world's richest reservoirs of untapped oil," known today as the tar sands (Pratt 1976, 33). Such was their promise that government geologists ranked the tar sands among the chief assets of the Dominion, noting they would "add materially to the public wealth" of Canada (McConnell 1893). Consequently, the federal government was fully aware of the extent of the tar sands at the time, recognizing the petroleum

field as "the most extensive in America, if not the world." Despite reports of the desperate condition of the First Nations peoples in the northwest that were circulating around Ottawa for more than twenty years following Confederation, federal authorities began to show an interest in treaty with Athabasca's First Nations and Métis only in the late 1890s, right around the time of the discovery of gold in the Yukon. Finally, in 1899, the government entered into treaty negotiations with the inhabitants of the Athabasca Delta region, including the Cree (now known as MCFN) and Chipewyan (now known as ACFN) people of Fort Chipewyan.

For their part, Cree leaders were apprehensive about entering into treaty, because they believed that making a treaty would lead to interference with the hunting and trapping upon which they depended (McCormack 1984, 88). In light of their concerns, the Cree were given assurances that their access to traditional lands would not be restricted and that they would be able to continue subsistence hunting unimpeded. Consequently, in 1899, the Cree agreed to enter into treaty with the primary aim of preserving their subsistence economy and traditional mode of production, and to protect their way of life. The treaty contained several promises from the government, including payments in cash and goods; the right to fish, hunt, and trap in certain areas; access to education and medical services; and an agreement to create reserves in the future.[1] Thus, only because of the significant potential for future resource development and imminent immigrant influx from the Klondike gold rush did the government briefly abandon its laissez-faire approach. Even if the Cree had previously sought to enter into treaty, the Canadian state was committed to a policy of proceeding with northern treaties only when the land was required for non-First Nations use. The state thus held the power to decide if and when treaty discussions would take place.

Treaty 8 had two significant political effects. First, it politically segregated the local indigenous population by creating legal entities called "Indian bands," which led to the establishment of separate and distinct administrative units. Although the federal government had previously made a formal division between Indian and non-Indian under the terms of the Indian Act of 1876, the process of treaty making with the Fort Chipewyan populations marked the beginning of the formalization of local political, social, and economic distinctions between treaty and non-treaty Indians.[2] The second effect of the treaty was that it expanded the potential scope for federal involvement in and jurisdiction over Cree land. Although the federal government had already been assigned responsibility for "Indians" in s. 91 (24) of the 1867 Constitution Act, under Treaty 8, the federal government assumed even more control.

Significant, therefore, is that in the early post-treaty years the government refrained from overextending itself in the sphere of Cree governance, restricting its involvement to minimal oversight of local affairs, primarily through the imposition of federal hunting regulations. Despite the formalization of the Crown-Cree relationship, Treaty 8 left traditional Cree governance largely unaffected.

The Return to Laissez-Faire

Government supervision of the Cree in the early post-treaty years can be described as fairly lax. Federal focus remained primarily on the restriction and regulation of hunting and trapping to support the economic initiatives of entrepreneurs in the region. The treaty itself represented an exceptional and limited interventionist move to deal with a potential impediment to imminent settlement and resource development. Yet the treaty had no obvious impact on Cree governance, and traditional leadership persisted into the post-treaty years. During this period, the Cree remained fairly independent, making their own decisions, until government authority was eventually imposed through state agents.

Traditional First Nations governance was effectively provided by band council governance mechanisms. In 1900, there were four systems of band government in Canada: the three-year elective system (Indian Act), the one-year elective system (Advancement Act), the hereditary system (in the North), and the appointment system (mainly in the prairies) (Dickason 1992, 321). Under this regime, some bands on the Prairies "were allowed to continue selecting their chiefs by their traditional methods. The department, in approving the chiefs so selected, regarded them as appointees" (ibid.). In other instances, bands simply "elected" hereditary chiefs as a way to circumvent the imposition of new norms and procedures and maintain traditional governing practices. Cree traditional leadership endured, provided by good hunters who could provide for the group.

Expansion and Intervention in the Postwar Period

Prominent thinkers of the postwar era showed a profound distrust of the market economy. In the wake of the Great Depression of the 1930s, scholars such as the economist John Maynard Keynes struggled to find a way to control global markets "by making them work for people and not the other way around" (Ellwood 2001, 25). In his famous work, *The General Theory of Employment, Interest and Money* (1936), Keynes argued "that the free market, left on its own, actually creates unemployment" (quoted in Ellwood 2001, 24). To "prime the economic pump," Keynes advocated the extension of the role of the state to correct the failings of the market. That is, he suggested that governments intervene actively in the economy. He suggested that when the economy was in a tailspin, it was up to "governments to act and step in by spending on public goods like education, health care, job training, roads, dams, railways [and] by wading in with direct financial support to the unemployed through social transfer payments like welfare and unemployment assistance" (Ellwood

2001, 26). Even if governments had to go into debt to spark economic growth, Keynes advised politicians not to worry, because the price was worth it. As the Second World War wound down, government policy makers who wanted to ensure a smooth transformation to a peacetime economy embraced the Keynesian solution of an interventionist state. It was Keynes' radical notion to which governments, including the Canadian one, turned in an effort to set their economies back on a steady keel.

Northern Development and the Crown-MCFN Relationship

After the Second World War, the Canadian government abandoned its laissez-faire stance and began institutionalizing Keynesian state planning and intervention. The government responded to changes in the global economic order by creating a central but different role for the Canadian state. Through increased social spending, the government dramatically altered its role in society. Through expanded jurisdictional control, it intensified its intervention in the lives of its citizens and First Nations people.

Though somewhat removed from the war itself, Aboriginal people were not isolated from the postwar development effort. A new era of government expansion led to new ideas about the role of Aboriginal policy. More specifically, the focus of the government changed; the "integration and equality of opportunity became the guiding themes of new Indian policies throughout Canada, including the north" (McCormack 1984, 400). Government regulated economic development and the economy primarily through private enterprise and redistribution of income. Social programming aimed at opening up northern regions for exploration and exploitation to incorporate the North into a postwar economy supported by "generous government investment and subsidy to stimulate the exploitation of northern resources" (ibid., 399). Although the federal and provincial governments had different interests and projects, they were motivated by similar considerations. Consequently, there was convergence between their diverse efforts. As the federal government sought to shift its national vision northward and initiate a second stage of national expansion, so too did the province of Alberta, seeking to open northern regions to exploitation and expansion.

Essential to this expansion was state intervention. The federal government encouraged industry to move into the Fort Chipewyan region. It also developed a host of new institutions to support northern industry development. For instance, in 1953, Parliament created the Department of Northern Affairs and National Resources to emphasize the importance of northern Canada and its economic development. This new department represented a shift from minimal government oversight to accelerated intervention designed to develop the national, northern, and Aboriginal economies rapidly. The department's underlying focus on the protection and assimilation of Aboriginal people led to its increased control over them.

The Role of the Indian Agent

A crucial intermediary in the expansion of federal control and jurisdiction was the Indian Agent. Over time, the increased control and authority of this local representative of the federal government undermined traditional Indian authority and leadership.

The Indian Agent had two main roles. First, he functioned as the broker or intermediary between Ottawa and Fort Chipewyan. This required him to relay requests from the chief to superiors in Ottawa, where decisions were made. Second, the Agent implemented programs designed to accelerate First Nations assimilation. To that end, the Agent attended to administrative duties that included providing limited social assistance, such as deciding who would be sent away for medical treatment. The level of control and responsibility of the Agent transformed his role from broker to the more encompassing and powerful role of patron (McCormack 1984, 349).

Nevertheless, the Agent in Fort Chipewyan did not intervene significantly in local affairs before the Second World War, and MCFN governance remained unimpeded, with the rare exception of the enforcement of criminal statutes and, after the formation of Wood Buffalo National Park (1922-26), hunting and trapping violations. Yet even after 1932, when an Agent was officially installed in Fort Chipewyan, "the reality of his situation was that he was isolated in a northern community where he had considerable range for interpretation of departmental directives" (McCormack 1984, 349). While the Agent could have possessed a significant degree of autonomy and enlightenment, enabling him to promote and protect Cree values and traditional ways of life, he usually functioned as the voice of the federal government to MCFN. In effect, the Indian Agent worked in accordance with government directives.

In the Treaty 8 region, the government was less concerned with assimilating the Aboriginal population than with helping them to remain financially independent. In the northern context, this meant supporting the fur trade. The Agents at Fort Chipewyan thus used their powers to interpret laws to fit the local situation and support the Cree and Chipewyan people. This support enabled First Nations people to remain in the bush and not move into the town settlement, where they would have to live with the Agent's assistance (McCormack 1984, 278). Initially, the Agent was able to uphold the right of MCFN to hunt and trap within the boundaries of the national park. A significant effect of Indian Agent intervention, therefore, was the protection and promotion of the fur trade economy and the trapper lifestyle. Although the Agents had some success on the local level, they could not protect the Aboriginal hunters and trappers from the outside forces that would eventually threaten their way of life.

The process of transforming MCFN governance began in earnest after the Second World War, largely through the Agent. The Agent's activities began to undermine traditional leadership and authority significantly. In many ways, he became a "super chief," promoting the ideologies, policies, and goals of his superiors and transforming federal policy and directives into local plans of action. Jack (Jock) Stewart was one such Agent. Appointed to Fort Chipewyan in 1944, he became a powerful patron within the community. The archetypal "super chief," Stewart was particularly influential because he spoke the local languages and was knowledgeable about the area, having formerly served as a park warden. Stewart's influence was also acute, because of the duration of his presence in the community: his service lasted almost thirty years, ending only with his retirement in the early 1970s. During his tenure, Stewart functioned as an integral part of the community and worked effectively to influence cultural change in specific directions (Prentice 1998, 209).

During this time, the powers of the Agent grew such that Stewart performed four main roles. First, he functioned as the broker or mediator between government and the Cree. In this capacity, he mediated disputes between the Cree and the park administration and warden service and conveyed information about park regulations and trapping restrictions to MCFN. He also advised the Cree of their rights, often speaking on their behalf at trials.

Second, he continued to provide social assistance to the local people. This role grew substantially and encouraged dependency. For example, Stewart decided which people should be sent out of the community for medical treatment and which should be referred to the local mission to be seen by the nurse. But Stewart's role of providing social assistance also included the provision of shelter and financial/income assistance to the community. For instance, in 1945, Stewart began to dispense the family allowance and old age security benefits. To qualify for family allowance, children of First Nations families had to be attending school and living at home in the settlement. This economic incentive marked the beginning of mothers leaving traditional bush settlements and taking up residence in Fort Chipewyan.

As the Cree moved from the bush to the town, Stewart's influence expanded to include a third important role: developing the infrastructure and facilities to run programs. For instance, to meet growing housing demands, Indian Affairs began a residential housing program in 1958-59 (deCardinale 1996, a-34). The government provided funding for the construction of the houses, favouring settlement where services were already available. Through this program, Indian Affairs became the principal landowners of Crown lots in Fort Chipewyan on behalf of the Cree band. In 1955, Stewart introduced state health care to the community, setting up nursing services in the Indian Affairs office (ibid., a-22). Shortly thereafter, in 1958, the first free-standing health centre/nursing station opened. As a result, the Cree people shifted their residence from the bush to Fort Chipewyan to access important and much-needed medical, educational, and financial assistance provided through Indian Agent Stewart.

Stewart's fourth and final role was to foster Cree education. Although Treaty 8 made the federal government responsible for the education of First Nations students, government-sponsored education was virtually absent in Fort Chipewyan until the 1940s (Vermillion 1991, 24). As a result, Stewart began to encourage education for First Nations children since education was crucial to the government's postwar northern policy. It was also the major instrument of culture change for the local First Nations population. The focus on education was soon followed by an amendment to the Indian Act in 1951 that made education compulsory. In the 1950s, the government was directly involved in the local administration of education. Education in the community became secularized when, in 1958, the Department of Indian Affairs built a public school adjacent to the mission school. Although the federal government still delivers schooling in many First Nations communities, in 1960, the Province of Alberta established Northland School Division no. 61 and assumed responsibility for the administration of education in Fort Chipewyan. This meant that the control and direction of education was transferred from Indian Affairs in Ottawa to the Department of Education in Edmonton, eliminating an important element of federal power in the community.

During this period, the First Nations people themselves were politically assertive; but their best efforts did not solve the main dilemma they faced – their lack of control over their means of production and over their institutions. The Cree had to act within a framework of non-First Nations economic, political, and social domination. Hence, the postwar era is significant in the history of Crown-MCFN relations because the state expanded its control over the Cree people. Through Stewart, the relationship was fundamentally transformed. As an Indian Agent, Stewart became an important instrument for social and economic change and a supporter of the welfare ideology. The consequence of intervention by the Indian Agent was an interdependent system of Indian status persons and government administration (McCormack 1984, 348).

Neoliberalism and the Post-Treaty Land Entitlement
In the early 1980s, the government of Canada created a Third National Policy (TNP) that included hemispheric economic integration, market-driven development, and a reduced role for the state, especially in the provision of social welfare. As Brodie (1997b) explains, "the new logic of the TNP is that nation-states must now abandon their role as buffer and force national economies to adjust to stark realities of the market and global competition" (255). This policy hollowed out the Keynesian welfare state to make way for market solutions and a corporate-centred future. But the transformation of the state did not diminish its role in Fort Chipewyan but instead shifted it, as evidenced in its policies promoting retrenchment. For instance, the neoliberal ideology required a new development strategy, a new approach

to public policy making, and a new approach to the management of state-citizen relations. This shift ultimately led government to negotiate a new relationship with First Nations people, one premised on the resolution of outstanding claims that threatened the potential for economic growth and the stability of the development environment.

In the early 1980s, alternative ideas about the relationship between First Nations and the state began to emerge in various forms of policy advice to the government (Weaver 1990, 15). These ideas fortuitously corresponded with First Nations pleas for a renegotiated relationship with the state. For instance, state intervention was identified as an impediment to First Nations development, and thus it was necessary for the state to alter its relationship with First Nations people. This led both the federal and provincial governments to decentralize power and download control to First Nations governments. As one provincial official stated, "the whole notion of delegating and bringing responsibility to the community level, that's good" (Interview with provincial government representative 2000c). This, in turn, led to a new era in First Nations administration, one that saw a reduction in federal constraints and a corresponding increase in First Nations responsibility for program delivery.

The advent of neoliberalism in the 1980s also created an important paradigm shift "away from the tight control and hierarchical relationship to more recognition of First Nations communities with rights of jurisdiction" (Prince and Abele 2002, 9-10). Though it can be argued that the shift began in the 1970s in federal policy regarding First Nations self-determination, the neoliberal 1980s is a more convincing starting point for this change, because government policy was shifting to suit global economic imperatives.

The new directions in First Nations policy introduced in the 1980s also reflected new thinking about First Nations issues. As it became clear that First Nations problems were tied to federal and provincial policies that impeded First Nations market participation, the removal of government regulations and restrictions was the obvious antidote. The new policy approach reflected the notion that First Nations people could best redress their dependent condition themselves. By changing the definition of the problem – from needing state protection to eliminating state barriers to market participation and socioeconomic development – the shift from paternalism to partnership makes sense.

Resource Development and the Treaty Land Entitlement
State retrenchment is not the only reason for the new direction in First Nations policy. Other stimuli are encouraging federal and provincial governments to settle outstanding land claims, especially those in resource-rich areas. For instance, increased resource development in northern Alberta stimulates land claim settlements.

The potential for a Cree challenge to all-important energy revenue was a serious threat that spurred the negotiations behind its specific claim, or treaty land entitlement. The 1969 *Statement of the Government of Canada on Indian Policy* (also known as the White Paper) had advocated abandoning federal responsibility for First Nations. Backlash to it and to the Calder case led to a policy reversal in which the government expressed an interest in settling any outstanding land entitlements. Taking advantage of a new will to negotiate, the Cree put forward their land claim in 1971. Shortly thereafter, in 1973, the Cree and the federal government reached a preliminary TLE agreement, through which the Cree would receive a total 97,280 acres, based on the standard Treaty 8 formula of 128 acres per person.[3] In August 1974, they selected 42,000 acres at two locations in Wood Buffalo National Park (WBNP). That same month, they passed a band resolution requesting the federal government to advise the Alberta government of its intention to select the balance of the 97,280 acres in the tar sands area of northeastern Alberta (Young 1974, 1).

The inclusion of the Alberta government in the TLE process was necessary by virtue of the 1930 Natural Resources Transfer Act. Although WBNP was under federal jurisdiction, land no longer required for national park purposes automatically reverted to the provinces. The province was under obligation to provide land for reserves, since provincial consent was essential for the return to the federal government of lands needed to meet the terms of the TLE. The Cree thus acknowledged that if pushed too far, the province could "kill the deal" with the federal government, in which case they would not achieve a settlement.[4] Hence, TLE talks had to proceed on a trilateral, not bilateral, basis.

In February 1975, the Alberta government agreed to transfer the land to create reserves for MCFN. Despite federal requests and assurances of action, however, the province never complied. The province then complicated the negotiating process by refusing to use contemporary population figures to determine the entitlement. It announced that it would proceed only "on the basis of population count at the time of Treaty signing and the retention unto the province of (all) mines and minerals" (Hyndman 1978, 1). According to federal officials, the decision of the provincial government to repudiate the deal "appears to have been partly motivated by Alberta's concern that the band had indicated an intention to select the remainder of their entitlement lands in the Tar Sands," (Brown 1978, 1). Chief Waquan explains that "without any prior discussion, the province altered the fundamental terms of the settlement reached four years earlier" (Selin 1999, 16). Ultimately, the province's revised position led to an impasse. As the province remained steadfast that it was willing to transfer only 24,000 acres to MCFN, based on its population of 1899 and on the condition that MCFN accept the amount as its full and final entitlement, MCFN walked away from negotiations.[5]

Despite the demise of the deal, the federal government continued to seek a positive resolution to the MCFN entitlement claim. The federal government maintained that although questions of population count and mineral rights, if pursued, would have to be a matter for determination in the courts, it was willing to work with MCFN to meet and fulfill its duties and obligations set out under Treaty 8. Eventually, negotiations resumed in the early 1980s. At this point, the spirit of negotiations had changed. This was in large part due to the fact that MCFN had withdrawn its claim to the oil sands. Because the membership wanted a deal that would lay the foundation for the band's future economic self-sufficiency, and because the claim to the oil sands lands was at the centre of the impasse, MCFN leaders removed the oil patch lands from its claim and turned its attention to securing land (and cash in lieu of land) and the right to govern that land. In the band's view, "the goal of settling the outstanding treaty entitlement [was] to lay the foundation for the future economic self-sufficiency of the Cree Band," which required the resolution of a deal and not an enduring battle with the provincial government over the oil sands (Zaharoff 1982a, 2).

At a meeting in Fort Chipewyan on 6 May 1982, the band presented a new set of proposals to federal and provincial representatives. This document, *Principles and Proposals for Treaty 8 Entitlement Settlement,* expressed a desire to participate successfully in the economic changes taking place in the region to relieve dependency and poverty (Fort Chipewyan Cree Band 1982, 27). It also recommended that matters of social development be integrated with economic objectives and carried out concurrently with economic development. It explained how "attention must be given to the planning, operation and delivery of programs, services and facilities to attack the real causes of our dependency and to prepare and assist us in the slow, lengthy socialization process needed if we are to successfully participate in and profit from economic development prospects" (ibid., 28). The Cree insisted that social, political, and economic development were the band's priorities and the basis for negotiations. It linked economic self-sufficiency to increased levels of political autonomy, which in turn was tied to increased capitalization.

At that time, the Cree chief and council met with the Honourable Don Johnston, then federal minister of Intergovernmental Affairs, and two provincial ministers. As one band member noted, where once the government of Alberta had appeared to be an adversary, it now expressed support and interest in settling the treaty entitlement. A new deal was reached that would provide the Cree with 24,000 acres (later revised to 12,280 acres) of provincial Crown lands outside of WBNP and guarantee the transfer of mines and minerals on these lands *so long as they were not the tar sands* (Zaharoff 1982a, 1). An important obstacle to the timely settlement of the claim had been overcome by willingness to omit the oil sands from the claim. An important goal of the province had also been achieved, evident in its interest in settling the claim and ensuring unfettered resource development. The TLE was thus necessary to protect the integrity of Alberta's economy.

Since government concentrates on managing big economic decisions, through which it determines the rate of development of natural resources (which has been the essence of government policy since the nineteenth century), the TLE functions as one such economic decision. Nowhere is this more evident than in the province of Alberta, where support for the TLE was tied to ongoing support for resource development and a stable political environment that would facilitate resource expansion and increase important resource revenues.

Compelling proof is found in the policies of the Conservative Party, which has governed Alberta since 1971. Throughout its reign, the Conservative government deliberately and successfully assisted the private sector, fostering oil-related economic growth and wealth generation. For example, in 1975, Albertans were receiving ten times more revenues from natural resources than other Canadians, per person (Taft 1997, 115). In the 1980s, this amount reached thirty times the national per capita level. Taft explains that from "1971 to 1994, resource revenues received by the Alberta government were worth $75.8 billion," reaching about $81.5 billion in 1995 and 1996 (ibid.). Given the importance of oil-related growth and development in Alberta, resolved land claims were desirable, since they acted as an important stabilizing agent and economic development tool. That is, as the provincial government sought to increase revenues, it needed to relieve itself and the province of the potential for legal claims and political disruption by First Nations groups that might deter foreign investment. As one government report stated, "Unresolved land settlement issues create uncertainty around land and resource use and ownership, making it difficult to attract and maintain investment opportunities" (Working Group on First Nations Participation in the Economy 2001, 9).

Conclusion

The issue of resource development was central to the treaty land entitlement process for the MCFN. The MCFN claim to land in the oil sands was intimately connected with the provincial interest in protecting its interests in those lands. In addition, the deal centred on ensuring that the oil sands lands remained intact and that resource royalties remained beyond the reach of MCFN. The significance of the MCFN claim to lands in the oil patch therefore cannot be understated. This claim was critical for gaining government attention and generating provincial interest in the larger MCFN claim. By making themselves a potential obstacle to resource development, MCFN compelled the governments toward settlement.

The MCFN TLE fit well into the neoliberal agenda. It was only a matter of time before the state began to transfer control over programs and services to MCFN. Thus, the TLE marked a watershed in MCFN and led to the dramatic transformation of the community. This is most likely why most MCFN members identify the TLE as the crucial catalyst for their change.

4
The Politics of Change

The process of self-determination occurs in two dimensions: political and economic. While these dimensions are inextricably bound together in governance, it is best to consider them separately, since they each highlight shifts in Crown-MCFN relations and correspond to broader shifts in the national and international political economy.

MCFN politics were transformed when the TLE awarded 12,280 acres of land and $26.6 million, with the government of Alberta contributing the land and $17.6 million while the government of Canada contributed $9 million. Land allocation included nine reserve sites, including one in the west end of Fort Chipewyan, known as Doghead; a small reserve in the Wood Buffalo National Park at Peace Point; and one to the northeast of the settlement. The settlement also included hunting and trapping rights and re-affirmed 3 million acres in the southern portion of the national park as traditional lands. The land allocation was important because it provided MCFN with a land to govern. The money was also important, not just for symbolic reasons, but for the practical development of the economy and social programs. The cash infusion provided the means for starting new business ventures and financing community development. Ultimately, the land and cash awarded in the TLE laid the foundation for changes in MCFN decision-making ability and accountability. The TLE thus marked the beginning of the transformation of MCFN governance.

Since self-determination is economic as well as political, it is important to recognize that the TLE influence is directly economic and indirectly political. The settled claim is intimately linked with self-government, not only in terms of First Nations ownership and control over lands and shared management of resources, but also in many other realms of governance, including policy development and service delivery in fields such as health, housing, and education. The degree of self-determination available twenty years ago differs significantly from what is available now. What are these changes in governance? First and foremost was the development of a band philosophy that promoted economic development as a strategy for self-preservation.

The MCFN Governance Vision

To ensure that economic development took place within the context of the community, band goals for development reflected the goals and aspirations of the wider MCFN community. To that end, in 1990, the chief and council held a workshop to discuss the future of MCFN. Several community members known for their success in business, the professions, and the arts participated in the four-day discussion. The outcome was a mission statement that reflected a market-oriented approach to socioeconomic development:

> By the year 2000, our people will be independent, proud professionals, working co-operatively in a clean environment in such a way that we preserve our Treaty Rights, cultural and spiritual values, to enhance our self-esteem so that competent people of the Mikisew Cree First Nation will be conducting all Mikisew Cree First Nation business in all fields in Fort Chipewyan and on lands of the Mikisew Cree First Nation by having no people of the Mikisew Cree First Nation on welfare.
>
> The people of the Mikisew Cree First Nation see our future as being self-sufficient. Working together while practicing good planning [cultural and educational], resulting in the development of the lands of the Mikisew Cree First Nation and keeping our Indian rights [sic]. (Selin 1999, 9)

Designed to guide MCFN actions and chart a course for the future, the mission statement reflects MCFN members' understanding of the importance of self-sufficiency, self-determination, local ownership and authority, education, training, career development, healthy lifestyles, and community participation, all of which mirror their underlying social values, "parallel [with] those of any other community" (deCardinale 1996, j-1). Hence, the mission statement, officially referred to as the Vision 2000, is a statement of what MCFN perceives to be important and how it defines success.

The mission statement represents the guiding principles for all MCFN policies and institutions. It also represents a connection between the governance priorities of MCFN on the one hand and its social values on the other. More specifically, the mission statement informs all subsequent decision making and outlines program direction, allowing leaders to concentrate on certain policy issues. MCFN designs its government, operations, and corporate interests to achieve the statement's objectives. Because the statement is focused on the economy, it connects MCFN governance priorities with government and industry interests. More specifically, the goals in the MCFN vision parallel those of other stakeholder groups in regional economic development. For instance, the vision statement urges meaningful and long-term participation in the oil sands operations, which is a goal encouraged by industry and fostered by government. It also advocates increased control over programs and services as well as development of a local economic base and employment opportunities, all of which complement the government's need to reduce its role in the governance of First Nations (deCardinale 1996, j-3). Hence, the mission statement not only reflects a vision of the future but also reflects the confluence of interests between MCFN, the state, and the marketplace.

MCFN Governance

MCFN is governed by a chief and council (a total of six councillors) democratically elected for a term of three years. It holds democratic, fair, and open elections for leadership, in accordance with terms set out in an election regulations policy, with election day falling every three years on Treaty Day. The TLE did not extricate MCFN from the Indian Act; as a result, MCFN is still an Indian Act band; it is not a formal self-governing First Nation, as would have resulted from a modern treaty along the lines of the Nisga'a Final Agreement or from formal legislation, as in the case of the Sechelt.[1] But since the TLE, despite the constraints historically associated with Indian governance under the Indian Act, the role and function of the MCFN band council have noticeably expanded. As the federal government slowly begins to devolve program and policy to the band, MCFN begins to expand the scope of its governance.

Financing MCFN Governance

The TLE and the funds it provided the band are largely responsible for the expanded scope of MCFN governance. However, a change in the federal-First Nation fiscal relationship set out in the Canada/First Nation Funding Agreement (C/FNFA) also contributed to the change. The C/FNFA is a block-budgeted funding agreement that DIAND enters into with certain First Nations groups. The federal government provides funds to First Nations for a period of five years and transfers authority to First Nations for program design and delivery. In exchange, First Nations are required to provide a core set of services that meet minimum standards for local accountability. Since signing its own C/FNFA in the late 1990s, MCFN manages an approximately $25.7 million budget over five years and now possesses "greater authority to redesign programs and reallocate funds between programs in accordance with community priorities" (Williams 1991, 27).

The C/FNFA agreement is important to MCFN because of the degree of control it offers. The federal government awards greater authority to Aboriginal communities based on the type of federal-First Nation funding agreement it has. Another type, the Comprehensive Funding Agreement (CFA), is a fairly restrictive one-year arrangement. The CFA transfers money monthly from the federal government to the band as a reimbursement for actual expenditures. For instance, if a CFA band has 100 members on social assistance, CFA provides funds for 100. During the following month, if only ninety people require social assistance, then the band only receives compensation for ninety recipients. Under this arrangement, the federal government reimburses a band for its expenses; and at the end of the year, if there is any surplus of funds, the band is required to repay those monies.

In contrast, the C/FNFA provides a First Nation with a block transfer of funds in a multi-year arrangement (usually five years). Its primary attribute is its flexibility. A C/FNFA provides First Nations complete freedom to manage a global budget, as long as they meet the minimum terms and conditions of capital operations and maintenance, education, social services, and their administration. As one government agent explained, "Once they meet the limited terms and conditions, they have latitude to move that money around" (Interview with federal government representative 2000c). At the end of the year, if the band has a surplus in one specific area (for instance, if it has a surplus of half a million dollars originally marked for social assistance), the First Nation can reallocate those monies to address other needs in other areas (e.g., housing or post-secondary education). This also enables the First Nation to change policies and introduce its own procedures. For example, MCFN can introduce programs to foster employment instead of simply subsidizing social assistance dependence. According to federal officials, the key to this type of arrangement is that the band has more autonomy and control over how and where monies are spent.

Another feature of the C/FNFA-type agreement is that the base amount of funding adjusts annually in proportion to whatever increase INAC receives from the Treasury Board. In other words, budget increases that the Alberta Region receives to its base budget are passed on to First Nations through this multi-year agreement. However, if the band runs out of funds before the end of the five-year period, the federal government is protected by an indemnity clause that relieves it of any additional financial responsibility. Despite the fact that the C/FNFA means that the federal government will not provide a "bailout" to First Nations who mismanage funds, federal officials claim that they do not hide behind the indemnity clause. They concede that if a community had members that were not receiving their social assistance, the federal government would intervene to make sure the programs were being properly delivered.

Federal officials claim that the long-term aim of the change in fiscal arrangements is to move from a restrictive regime to a transfer type of agreement. Indeed, the C/FNFA is indicative of the government goal to reorient Aboriginal-state relations and First Nations fiscal relations away from paternalism and toward First Nations self-determination. First, it reflects a lack of interest on the part of the federal government to continue to strictly scrutinize and control the financial operations of First Nations. Hence, it reflects overarching neoliberal goals, using the C/FNFA to reduce its role in First Nations government and removing the burden of micromanagement.

Second, it reflects increased financial decision-making authority and independence for MCFN. As one member explains, "You get a block of funding. You manage it, move it around, and see how it fits. That is why we are starting to be more independent. Before, we used to have to live by their [government] rules" (Interview with MCFN member 2000i).

With increased authority, however, comes increased accountability. Under C/FNFAs, the chief and council are accountable in two ways. First, they must answer to their membership for the quality of their leadership, sound management of council affairs, and efficient and effective delivery of departmentally funded services; and, second, they must answer to the federal government for use of public funds used to carry out program objectives. More specifically, the C/FNFA terms and conditions include provisions to ensure financial health is maintained and internal financial controls are in place and in accordance with generally accepted accounting principles. Finally, C/FNFAs require annual audits and performance reports for DIAND and community members. MCFN continues to formalize existing accountability mechanisms for its members and for the funds and services it manages on their behalf. It is compliant in providing financial audits and reports to the government (DIAND 2007). Although these constraints exist, they are minimal compared to previous funding arrangements and the strict scrutiny that accompanied them.

The ability of the MCFN chief and council to spend according to the community's own needs and priorities is an important change in MCFN governance. It enables them to mediate the demands of economic development and market participation with the needs of its membership. According to former chief Waquan, the key is to plan strategically, identify all the potential issues that may arise, and take them into account when negotiating the agreement. The C/FNFA is of historical significance for the people of MCFN, as he explains:

> It represents the achievement by my First Nation of recognition and respect from the Government of Canada for the ability of my people to govern their affairs in a prudent and proper manner. Most importantly, it also represents a major milestone that the Mikisew Cree First Nation has achieved toward the development of its self-government and ultimately, self-sufficiency through the positive enhancement of our people. The [C/FNFA] is a true expression of the commitment and dedication of my First Nation and the Government of Canada toward the realization of our goal of economic independence through accountable and responsible self-government. (DIAND 1996a)

With a large financial package as a part of the final TLE settlement, the band had the power to make important decisions.

Restructuring and Institutional Design

After the TLE, the MCFN underwent a period of organizational restructuring to manage the new challenges of economic development and political governance. The most significant change was the separation of band politics from band business and band administration. Prior to the TLE, elected band officials were responsible for band administration, including both political and economic development. After the TLE, these responsibilities were divided to protect business from politics and to separate economic development from political administration (since political administration was a critical element for political success). The result was the transformation of the daily administrative affairs of the band and the creation of a host of new positions, including the office of the chief executive officer, chief financial officer, economic development officer, director of social services, administrative manager, and director of education. For example, the CEO was to oversee five central departments: central administration, accounting services, community services, educational and training services, and technical services. The CEO also had to ensure that the band met its goals in program delivery, met the needs and the expectations of its membership, and remained accountable to the chief and council and the membership. By being directly accountable to the community, MCFN leadership further ensured that the band's business activity complemented and supported the long-term goals of the band. Direct accountability to the community and commitment to realizing the terms of the mission statement ensured that the land claim monies were used to support the growth and development of the community.

But market imperatives also influenced this separation of band governance from band enterprise. MCFN made important institutional and structural changes at the behest of Syncrude, a local resource corporation. Syncrude advised MCFN to separate its political institutions from its economic institutions because it felt that the historical fusion of band-elected leaders and First Nations businesses created difficulty in its working effectively with the band and its companies. According to Syncrude officials, the mix of politics and business in the communities was a significant obstacle to working together: "One of the struggles that we had with the developing companies in the First Nations communities is that we had a hard time getting the band elected leaders to separate themselves from running the business. And every time the band council changed over, they would fire all the management in the company and then you would have to restart again, so we wanted to change that. We wanted to make sure that these companies were set up in a way that they could be managed irrespective of who the chief was" (Interview with Syncrude representative 2000b). Syncrude wanted to ensure that MCFN companies were set up in a way that they could be managed, notwithstanding the politics inherent in band administration. In exchange,

Syncrude promised that MCFN- or Cree-owned businesses would receive a significant portion of supply and service opportunities. It was clear that the corporate sector wanted to see a particular model of governance within the MCFN community. Archie Waquan, the chief at the time, acted in accordance with this directive and oversaw the extraction of band government from band business, and he attributed the success of the First Nation to a distinct division between political and administrative functions: "We keep politics to the politicians and administration to the administrators" (Selin 1999, 7).

The operation of MCFN businesses was subsequently placed under the control of the Mikisew Energy Services Group. MESG is 100 percent owned by the MCFN and includes three companies: 2000 Plus Limited Partnership, Mikisew Maintenance Limited Partnership, and MSD Limited Partnership. These businesses were formed to service the oil sands operations and, at the same time, provide economic opportunities (employment and skill development) for MCFN members. Almost 50 percent of the employees are Aboriginal, and most of them are from MCFN. "Originally, when we started, we were just supplying labour," reported Charles Iggulden, MESG president and CEO. "Then we started building houses." As the companies grew, they started doing heavy-machinery work, civil road construction, carpentry, facility construction, and plant maintenance. MESG now does about $10 million to $15 million worth of business each year (Wittchen 2004, 1).

Policy Development and Implementation

Changes in governance are apparent not only in organizational restructuring and governing philosophy but also in policy design and implementation. Kalt and Cornell (1992) suggest that policy control is another important element of self-determination. They assert that informed, thoughtful policy making and effective, accountable institutions that implement community-directed policy are critical elements of self-determination. For MCFN, these elements are most evident in shifts in health, housing, and education policy. These three policy areas are also good indicators of the impact of the new political economy on local governance, because they show how previously interrelated levels of government functioned and how the shift to local/MCFN control of them has occurred. These three policy areas also demonstrate change in the ways the social needs of the community are assessed and evaluated, met and administered (see Table 2). Considering each of them constitutes a sector-specific approach to self-determination as opposed to comprehensive or legislative self-determination.

Health

Over the past decade, the federal government has transferred responsibility for many health services to the community level. The devolution of health care recognizes not only the centrality of local government but

Table 2

MCFN governance transformation, pre- and post-treaty land entitlement, 1986

	Pre-treaty land entitlement	Post-treaty land entitlement
Land claim	No reserved lands	Reserves assigned and cash awarded
Financial arrangement	Annual funding arrangement	C/FNFA: multi-year block funding ($25 million every five years)
Housing	Three houses a year provided by INAC	MCFN develops own housing strategy and works with CMHC and own businesses
Health care	Provided by federal government Medical Services Branch (now FNIHB[1])	Provided by federal government via Nunee Health Authority
Education	Federal-provincial	Federal-IEA[2]-provincial
Market activity	Hunting/trapping/wage labour (seasonal, Syncrude/Suncor/Shell and government jobs)	MCFN businesses[3] and previous activities
Governance	INAC-MCFN (Indian Act and Treaty 8)	INAC-MCFN (Indian Act and Treaty 8)

Notes:
1 FNIHB = First Nations and Inuit Health Branch
2 IEA = Indian Education Authority
3 MCFN companies include (but are not limited to) Air Mikisew Ltd., Fort Chipewyan Building Supplies, Fort Petroleum Corporation, Mikisew Energy Services Group (2000 Plus, MSD, Mikisew Maintenance Limited Partnership), and Mistee Sepee Development Corporation.
Source: Mikisew Cree First Nation 1999; Mikisew Energy Services Group 2007.

also the administrative burden health care management poses to the federal government.

Historically, all health services provided to the Fort Chipewyan community were provided directly by the Medical Services Branch (MSB) of Health Canada through the local nursing station. This included physician and nursing services and dental and vision care. There were four nurses on staff, and physicians visited once every two weeks. All other services were very sporadic and infrequent, their quality was questionable, and they did not meet the needs of the community (Mercredi 2002). Without local control, there was no way for the community to participate in the planning, delivery, administration, or evaluation of health services. MSB (now known as the First Nations and Inuit Health Branch, or FNIHB) started transferring control of health services to First Nations and Inuit communities and organizations in the mid-1980s. In 1988, with the support of MSB, the Nunee (pronounced "New-knee") Health Authority was established at Fort Chipewyan.[2] A community-based initiative, Nunee faltered soon after starting, until it was eventually transformed into a more effective and accountable service centre under the leadership of Trish Mercredi. According to Mercredi, when she was hired in 1991, "There was me and $30,000. That was it. When I left in 1999 we had over 40 full-time employees, several buildings, a five-year agreement worth almost 29 million dollars, a continuum of health services, another agreement with the province, and almost total control of health services in the community" (Mercredi 2002). Although the desire to take control of health and to provide a consistent quality of health services that met the needs of the community had been present for some time, a combination of government will, community co-operation, and capable leadership coalesced to transform a long-term need into action. According to Mercredi, a lot of negotiating and effort was required to bring all parties (government, MCFN, ACFN, and Métis) together; but ultimately, she succeeded in convincing them that by working together and sharing financial resources, they could build a better health care system for everyone.

Nunee provides full local control over a range of health services, including regular physician visits, specialist services (i.e., pediatrician, gynecologist, ophthalmologist, occupational therapists, and so on), and regular mental health services with two therapists. The program has seven nurses and an elders' long-term care program. Additionally, it hosts a full range of community health activities, including a community wellness team, alcohol and drug addiction services on site, community-based training in areas such as addictions, suicide prevention programs, crisis management training, first aid courses, Health and Healing conferences, residential school training, summer healing camps, a health newsletter, a health status study, and a tele-health project.

The Telehealth Research Project is a good example of the improvements to local health through local management. This project was established as a partnership project between the Nunee Health Authority, the Northern Lights Regional Health Centre (NLRHC), TecKnowledge Health Care Systems Inc., and Health Canada. During a needs assessment, the community identified three health priorities: rehabilitation services (physical, speech, and occupational therapy), distance education for health providers, and support to hospitalized family members. Based on the needs assessment and funded by Health Canada, the Nunee Health Authority Telehealth Research Project was born. The program is one of the six pillars of the national Connectedness Agenda, which is designed to make Canada the most connected country in the world. Through it, community residents can communicate face-to-face with family members and health care professionals in the Fort McMurray hospital. Because it enables clients in the isolated community to receive speech therapy, physical therapy, and even occupational therapy without having to leave the community, the videoconferencing technology has been a crucial step in improving local health care. It has also alleviated the stress and cost of travel associated with medical treatment. An MCFN member explained the benefits of tele-rehabiliation: "When I had back problems, I had to fly to Fort McMurray for physical therapy, but the flights, and later the winter road travel for treatment, only made my back pain worse" (see Humenuk-Bourke 2000, 3). Finally, the project represents an innovative use of modern technology that enables the community to preserve important cultural ties, since it links the sick and their families, who may find themselves separated for an extended period of time due to health crises.

Today, through a memorandum of understanding with NLRHC, the Telehealth Research Project provides Tele-Visitation services so that patients from the community who are hospitalized at NLRHC in Fort McMurray may visit family and friends in Fort Chipewyan. These sessions assist the emotional well-being of patients. In one interview, a Cree elder expressed her appreciation for the new technology that enabled her to visit her sister who was in hospital in Fort McMurray (Interview with MCFN member 2000o). Mary Simpson of the Nunee Health Authority says there's a proved therapeutic value to having regular visits from family and friends during the health process. Tele-Visitation started in March 2000 when it linked elders hospitalized in Fort McMurray to elders back in the community. In its first three years, the program had 51 successful sessions, and approximately 177 family members and friends of patients had used Tele-Visitation.

Financially accountable to the federal government, Nunee does not rely on provincial support for any services, and so its relationship with the province is limited to those services that Nunee might purchase from the provincial health provider, NLRHC (e.g., environmental health). The Nunee Health Authority is governed by a board that makes policy decisions, approves budgets, and determines programs and services. The board, whose members are selected by each community group, represents MCFN, ACFN, and the Métis and non-Native population. Some claim that "community health has gone band controlled" (Interview with MCFN member 2000b); but until 2001 one representative from each First Nations group, one elder, and one youth sat on the board, for a total of five board members. A community-wide call for an elder and a youth representative is announced whenever a vacancy arises. The applicant must submit a one-page expression of interest. The board then selects one elder and youth from the pool of applicants. In 2001, however, the composition of the board changed to reflect MCFN demands for greater representation based on its population. MCFN now has two representatives on the board, for a total of six board members. Given the demographic domination of MCFN in Fort Chipewyan, it wields significant power, both on the board and within the community. One federal government representative stated in an interview that Fort Chipewyan is a "Cree-dominated community [in part because] they have done very well and are highly organized," which leads to the perception that it is MCFN, not the board, that has ultimate authority over the operation of the health authority (Interview with federal government representative 2000a).

This view was reinforced in 2001 when MCFN threatened to withdraw its support from the health authority, charging it with failure to meet the special health needs of its elders, lack of leadership, and general mismanagement. MCFN suggested that it would take control over the administration of health services for its members. According to one health provider, this proved to be a point of great controversy, not only for the community but also for the federal government, which did not want to see the authority fall apart. The federal representative quoted above explained that few First Nations communities with so many different groups have been awarded control over health care and that this community has done very well. She added that "these are growing pains, and there isn't a similar community in Canada that has gone to transfer that is trying to please so many bands" (ibid.). That is, few bands that have taken the reins over the provision of health care have had to service three different First Nations groups within the same community. Consequently, given its demographic, political, and economic clout, if MCFN were to pull out of the arrangement, the future of the health authority would be jeopardized. Fortunately, this conflict was resolved by meeting MCFN demands for increased board representation, leaving the Nunee Health Authority intact.

According to one health care provider, the willingness of government to devolve control of health care service delivery and management indicates that "government wants out of health care of First Nations" (Interview with federal government representative 2000a). This sentiment was echoed by one MCFN member, who observed that "health is changing because there are a lot of things in health now that MSB wants people to pay for. There are a lot of prescription drugs that used to be covered and are not covered any more" (Interview with MCFN member 2000k). Other changes include longer time periods for prescription eye care (from a new pair of glasses every year to one every four years) and oral care renewal (from new dentures every two years to new dentures every five years) (ibid.). Overall, there is a sense within the community that the government is cutting back its services to First Nations people and that MCFN must fight to protect its treaty right to health care. MCFN concerns over the level of health care services its members receive reflect a larger concern that the federal government is trying to renege on its treaty obligations. As former chief Archie Waquan asked the Royal Commission on Aboriginal Peoples (RCAP) commissioners, "Is the government's attempt at getting out of their obligation ... a true indication of the government's commitment to encouraging the Mikisew Cree First Nation in becoming self-sufficient and independent?" (Waquan 1992, 21). In its defence, the federal government maintained that it is not, in any way, trying to abrogate its treaty responsibilities. One federal representative explained:

> We have responsibilities to First Nations. We are prepared to honour those responsibilities. We want to see self-sufficient, accountable First Nations evolve that have certain powers that are harmonious with federal and provincial powers. We want to see them involved with the private sector. I mean, the idea that Indian Affairs and the federal government, at least under this government – I mean, under previous governments there was the White Paper and that sort of thing – but I don't see it coming back. There are certain obligations the Crown has, and even if we wanted to, I think we would have a lot of difficulty getting out of those obligations [because] they are legal. (Interview with federal government representative 2000d)

Yet concern in the community persists over the extent to which devolved authority to the community could detract from federal treaty responsibilities.

Most MCFN members appear generally pleased that the community of Fort Chipewyan has effectively and efficiently taken the reins of health care from government. Although some fear that community-based health care detracts from the treaty right to health care, the transfer of jurisdiction from the federal government to the First Nation does not eliminate federal treaty responsibility to MCFN. The treaty does not specify who provides the service, just as long as the service is provided.

Housing

MCFN housing policy and practices reflect its transition to a joint public-private approach to the provision of services. These policies and practices also reflect one of neoliberalism's key goals: to transform everything into commodity form, with private property owned individually rather than collectively. In essence, after years of inadequate housing, a lack of reserve lands, and other setbacks, MCFN started seeking market-based solutions to its housing crisis. This required working in partnership with all stakeholders (MCFN members, band council, federal government, and private sector). The goal was to create new approaches to housing on-reserve that would bring about an overall and sustained improvement in housing conditions.

In 1992, MCFN launched its new housing initiative. It made the housing issue a priority and resolved to spend the majority of housing dollars on new construction. Though the TLE was settled in 1986, the survey of reserve lands did not take place until 1989. Once a land base was established, MCFN began to concentrate on providing housing. To date, it remains focused on the development of the new Allison Bay Reserve, a five-minute drive to the north and east of the townsite of Fort Chipewyan.

The C/FNFA was critical to new housing development because it spans several program areas. The federal government provided an additional $566,800 under the new federal housing policy announced in 1996, in addition to the $360,500 yearly housing allocation (DIAND 1996a). By the end of the eight-year project, which was completed in 2003, MCFN had committed approximately $4 million of the band's annual revenue toward the community's housing program. The goal to develop Allison Bay Reserve as the centre of the community required the construction of 78 units and the renovation and relocation of 161 houses. Houses and renovations were allocated by the housing committee, a group of seven MCFN members chosen and appointed by the chief and council to review requests.

The C/FNFA funding is a major departure from previous arrangements, wherein the federal government provided only enough funds to MCFN for the construction of three houses per annum. As one MCFN member put it, "If you look at how many people need housing here – I think there was 110 last time I looked – and you get three houses a year – and in my home alone I have my daughter and her kids living with me, and my uncle living with me because they don't have a house" (Interview with MCFN member 2000k). A new arrangement was needed not only because federal funding was insufficient but also because the funding was part of a federal campaign to transform the First Nations mindset that housing is "free" and a "right" enjoyed by First Nations people. As one federal representative commented, "It's the government's view that it [housing] is not a right. We are not going to provide money for housing for everybody on reserve. The government view of the First Nation communities is that if you are working and you have a job, maybe the First Nation community can help you to get started, but after that, you should be paying rent or a mortgage." The federal government cannot afford "to provide a free house, fully paid for by the government to every First Nation in Canada [because] you are talking billions of dollars" (Interview with federal government representative 2000d). Today, however, federal monies subsidize the construction of new houses.

Additionally, INAC encourages First Nations to work with other agencies to meet their housing needs, including the Canada Mortgage and Housing Corporation (CMHC). MCFN has been aggressive in taking advantage of programs offered by CMHC. It now has access to a mortgage assistance program that provides low-interest loans to members who qualify for a mortgage from a conventional financial institution. Once the houses are built, community members put their name on a list to request one. The housing committee reviews this list and, according to one member, assigns houses to those they deem most needy. Given their need to build eight or nine houses per year, and given the limitations of INAC funding, MCFN now requires people to pay rent for their property to cover the mortgage, as set out in the CMHC Home Ownership Incentives Program. With the exception of a few homes built for elders under the MCFN Social Housing Program, members living in houses constructed since 1992 are encouraged to either rent or buy their homes. By having members contribute to the cost of housing for today, the First Nation is ensuring that funds for housing will be available for future generations.

To compensate for income differences, the band often builds the house and then assumes the mortgage. It later sells the new house to a member, whose monthly mortgage payments take the form of "rent" to the band, which is prorated according to the purchaser's income. For instance, the maximum rent for a person on social assistance for a four-bedroom house is $510; and for a two-bedroom house or apartment, it is $325 (Mikisew Cree First Nation 1996). MCFN retains the right of first refusal in instances when the owner wishes to sell the house. While the band has been careful to make housing affordable, it has made members understand that there is no such thing as "free" housing.

But the transition from free housing to owning and renting housing can be difficult. Many MCFN members are unfamiliar with the obligations associated with renting. As one MCFN member commented, "People are used to not paying rent. The houses [were] owned by Indian Affairs. I am living in a house that was given to me by Indian Affairs, and I don't pay rent. Just the last few years with CMHC, we are having the problem. On reserve, they all pay rent, and we are having one helluva time to collect" (Interview with MCFN member 2000i). Another member added, "Some people don't understand. They think they should get it for nothing" (Interview with MCFN member 2000k). As First Nations take on more responsibility for local services and develop new partnerships and programs, they must deal with the pressures associated with new responsibility and with the re-education of their own people.

MCFN's physical ability to build and renovate housing further assists the housing program. MCFN created Fort Chipewyan Building Supplies, a business that provides building materials to the building company Mikisew Technical Services (MTS). MTS is also owned by MCFN and builds First Nation housing at cost. This partnership enabled MCFN to build a 950-square-foot, three-bedroom unit for $95,000 in 1996 (Palmer 1996, 1).[3] This arrangement enables MCFN to get the most out of its building dollars. Other MCFN companies provide necessary services to homes in the Fort Chipewyan community, including water services, sewer services, and fuel.

In these ways, MCFN has taken a proactive and entrepreneurial approach to addressing its housing crisis. Since 1992, MCFN has developed innovative ways to ensure that it is able to correct the shortcomings in previous housing programs and policies. For instance, for those who do not wish to live on-reserve, preferring to reside in the village of Fort Chipewyan, MCFN awards two $45,000 start-up grants per year to function as down payments for band members who want to build. This is another strategy designed by the band to alleviate the housing crunch. With clear direction from the chief and council, professional planning assistance, high-quality construction by MTS, and com-petitively priced materials from Fort Chipewyan Building Supplies, MCFN has been able to build cost-effective, high-quality homes for its members. Housing thus represents an important new policy direction. It is no longer about state provision of housing or band provision of housing but about individual own-ership in partnership with the band or the private sector.

Education

Education remains an area where there has only been a nominal change or decentralization of authority to MCFN. In conjunction with ACFN, MCFN sought increased control over the delivery of education in 1985, when it formed the Indian Education Authority (IEA), a board composed of three MCFN members and three ACFN members (Vermillion 1991, 29).[4] In 1987, the IEA signed a tripartite tuition agreement with the federal and provincial gov-ernments. When asked why the federal government agreed to transfer control for the administration of education dollars to the band, one government offi-cial responded, "That is part of devolution, transferring greater responsibility to the First Nation" (Interview with federal government representative 2000d). However, the level of responsibility transferred was negligible.

Under the terms of the agreement, the IEA had two roles. First, it had to administer the tuition agreement by managing funds transferred from the federal government to the band and to pay the province for educational services provided through the provincially regulated Athabasca Delta Community School, located in Fort Chipewyan.[5] Essentially, the IEA functioned as an intermediary between two orders of government, taking money from one to pay the other; and the delegated authority was limited to the doling out of education dollars. The outcome of the tuition agreement, therefore, was not increased control over education but increased financial management responsibility. Though MCFN and ACFN wanted more control over the delivery of primary and secondary education, the transfer of educational responsibility from the federal government to the local First Nation was insignificant. It did not translate into a more practical role for the bands in the provincially operated education system.

Second, the IEA was assigned the job of monitoring and reviewing the quality of education being delivered to band members in Fort Chipewyan. As one member explained, "The biggest challenge [is] trying to get our people educated" (Interview with MCFN member 2000g). The IEA recognized a number of issues related to the state of education in the community: a lack of achievement, poor reading skills, lack of discipline, poor attendance, and inadequate facilities and resources (no science or reading resource centres). Although the IEA prepared a report of its findings and delivered it to the province, no changes occurred. Even though MCFN pays the province close to $9,500 per student, the teachers continually complain that they are running out of materials well before the school year is over. At the high school level, a lack of teachers and the fact that most of the high school education is done through correspondence from Edmonton means that few students graduate.[6] Some parents have had to move to Fort McMurray to ensure that their children receive an adequate high school education. Other MCFN members recount stories of how they were sent away in order to be educated. These events indicate that the educational needs of MCFN members are not being met within the existing system.

Federal officials concede that MCFN students are not progressing well, admitting that "they are generally two grades behind" (Interview with federal government representative 2000d). Although the federal government funds First Nations education, MCFN identifies the problem as the delivery mechanism, which is the provincially operated school in Fort Chipewyan. Accordingly, "the chief from Mikisew met with the minister of Alberta learning and basically said here are the facts, you are running the system, we are paying you for our kids, and they are not being educated. We have to make some changes" (ibid.). Most First Nations have a school on-reserve that is run by the First Nation. The federal government provides these bands with money to operate the schools, hire the teachers, set the curriculum, and meet minimum provincial standards (ibid.). Hence, the federal government has suggested that the MCFN, ACFN, and the Métis join together to run a community school. As one federal official explained, "They will be accountable then. They can't blame anybody then because they will be running it" (ibid.). But when asked if MCFN should work to take control over education, one MCFN member suggested more immediate concerns must be addressed first: "When you consider the poverty that many of our people live in, [it doesn't] allow people the quality of a home life to ensure that people complete their education. [As long as] people have to worry about what kind of food they are going to eat and how they are going to pay their bills, economics will determine their quality of life" (Interview with MCFN member 2000q). In short, MCFN money, time, and attention is focused on addressing the essential lack of adequate medical care and housing, rather than on education. Unfortunately, the failure of MCFN to take control of education, which is essential to its economic development, may undercut its transformation to economic and political independence.

For its part, the IEA acknowledges that education is an important way to advance people's position in the marketplace. MCFN members also recognize that the problem of First Nations education is tied to economic opportunity. As one elder reasons, it is important for "kids to go to school to get an education ... because you have to have an education in order to have a job" (Interview with MCFN member 2000o). Local industry echoes this logic. Because Syncrude has set the completion of Grade 12 as the standard minimum qualification for jobs, it remains concerned about the problems in the local educational system. One area of specific concern is the low scores on achievement tests. For this reason, industry officials are investing money and time to improve educational opportunities for First Nations peoples. But Syncrude's altruism is motivated by more than a desire to educate: it wants to produce more workers. When asked if oil companies would be interested in taking over education, one industry official pointed out that German corporations have long been involved in education: "Now corporate Germany is really involved in education – like companies like Kroeger, they run their own schools – but they also have a very different system there. Here you kind of stream into becoming an engineer, or whatever. In Germany, if you want to be involved in metals, you all start off becoming welders. Some will stay welders, some will go on to become engineering technologists and metal engineer technologists, and out of that bunch some will go on to become mechanical engineers, but they all start off learning the basics together, which is a very interesting system" (Interview with Syncrude representative 2000a). He speculated that perhaps under the right conditions, industry involvement in education would be greater: "Would companies take over education? This isn't official, [but] they probably would if we didn't have to pay the education tax to the provincial government and we got the pick of people who graduated." He added, "Our educational programs are out of touch with corporate needs. It is wonderful to graduate thousands of people with philosophy degrees, but they aren't going to work anywhere. We need tradesmen, we need engineers." Another official noted, "No doubt the biggest challenge we have is that 54 percent of the Aboriginal population in this region is under twenty or twenty-five. We have a whole bunch of jobs coming open, all kinds of jobs – and there's no skill match (Interview with Syncrude representative 2000b). Given its pragmatism, industry has already become involved in educational initiatives in the region. For instance, Syncrude introduced a registered apprenticeship program for high school students that started in Fort McMurray and has spread throughout the province. The same official commented that through the program, "kids go to high school but they actually come and work for [us]." So as industry positions itself to take advantage of the education system, MCFN, along with other First Nations, must play a more active role in local education programming.

Conclusion

Events occurring in the international context may seem far removed from the relations between First Nations people and the state. Yet Canadian policy toward First Nations people mirrors global trends transforming the international system and also changing traditional understandings of the state-society relationship. A new direction in First Nations policy indicates that the state wants to transform its role with respect to First Nations people. Less federal scrutiny and more MCFN autonomy suggest that the political conditions for self-government have emerged. In the neoliberal era, therefore, it is apparent that MCFN self-determination has flourished as government control and management have diminished.

Critics of neoliberalism emphasize that it eliminates social programs and destroys progress made by underprivileged groups, and suggest that First Nations are particularly ill placed to resist the tide of globalization (see Angus 1990). Yet MCFN demonstrates that First Nations with the means to thrive in the marketplace can benefit from neoliberalism. At the same time, despite its economic success, MCFN's self-determination represents a specific neoliberal type of self-determination that remains limited in scope. MCFN is still a band under the Indian Act; thus, it lacks full and robust self-determination – authority based on inherency that is constitutionally protected and not delegated. As well, the extent to which MCFN exercises autonomous power versus delegated authority is debatable. MCFN's successes suggest that devolution can function effectively as de facto self-government policy, since decision-making power transferred away from the state is transferred to First Nations.

Notwithstanding the fact that devolved self-determination is not based on inherency and that many First Nations do not achieve their goals via devolution, devolution itself does not inhibit the eventual realization of those self-determination goals. Therefore, even though the assumptions guiding federal policy and activity may not reflect First Nations concepts of self-determination, devolution still facilitates the realization of First Nations goals of economic self-reliance and jurisdictional autonomy.

Prince and Abele (2002) suggest, however, that service delegation is not self-determination. They argue that in most service fields, "real decision making powers still today are not devolved" (10). At the same time, the new roles and responsibilities of the MCFN band government stand in stark contrast to the historical role of the federal government as the "custodial administrator" (10). This change is particularly welcome to MCFN, since the federal government has historically been perceived as a barrier for the First Nations people. As one member put it, "They [the government of Canada] are always trying to think for us but they could never think for us because we know what our needs are and we are the only ones that can help our people" (Interview with MCFN member 2000h).

Yet even when self-determination is narrowly defined to include only goals of political, social, and economic well-being, the power of self-governance in and of itself is no guarantee of economic development. The ability to manage, not just to administer, programs is important for creating an environment in which investors feel secure. The TLE thus provided MCFN not only an important base of capital, which enabled the band to be creative in its policy and its economic development, but also the environment that could make it happen.

5
The Economics of Change

The economic lens allows us to move beyond questions of *who decides* to questions of *who participates*, specifically in the marketplace. This chapter examines the extent to which the MCFN economy has been transformed, developed, and diversified, and explores the economic development experiences of the MCFN by answering two central questions. First, how much more participation in the market has occurred since the treaty land entitlement? Second, to what extent is MCFN a subject rather than object of economic activity? Enhanced capitalization, an important outcome of the TLE, is a critical factor in the increased economic development and market activity of MCFN. An amalgam of state policy and market opportunity has transformed the economic position of the MCFN. By comparing the level of economic development and the availability of opportunity twenty years ago with the current situation (specifically, the economic condition of MCFN both before and after the TLE), it is possible to identify these changes.

The Fur Trade: Market Penetration
During the colonial period, as the Europeans searched for new sources for raw materials and resources, they sought new markets for their manufactured goods. Upon arrival in Canada, Europeans discovered vast fur resources and recognized their economic potential. Though Innis (1927) wrote that the "importance of staple exports to Canadian economic development began with the fishing industry," it was the fur trade and the dominance of furs that led to the introduction of capitalism (401). The fur trade was significant not only because it drew Canada into the world economic system but also because it propelled the fur industry across the country and "drew a succession of Native economies into the European economic orbit" (ibid., vi). Consequently, the roots of First Nations economic participation and capitalist integration are in the mercantilist relationship of the fur trade, largely because of the central role First Nations played in it. As fur producers and traders, they were integrated into the European fur trade and made subject to its interests.

The Fur Trade and the Cree

The marketplace entered the Athabasca region when the Cree moved into the region around the middle of the seventeenth century, displacing the Beavers, Slaveys, and other tribes through warfare. As descendants of the Woodland Cree in eastern Canada, they became intermediaries for the Hudson's Bay Company (HBC). Anxious to break the HBC monopoly, the Montreal-based North West Company (NWC) arrived in the Athabasca region in 1778. Led by Peter Pond, the NWC immediately set up the trading post of Fort Chipewyan, which became "the most important North West Company post in the North" (Dickason 1992, 204). Fort Chipewyan was an important post because it was part of the new route connecting Hudson Bay with the Arctic drainage system. Ideally situated on the shores of Lake Athabasca, Fort Chipewyan was the final depot for all NWC trade destined to and from Montreal along the Peace, Athabasca, Slave, and other rivers in the Mackenzie basin. As a result of its monopoly in the region, the NWC dominated the northern fur trade here until the end of the eighteenth century.

In 1802, the HBC made its first attempt to take control of the region by establishing a small trading post in Fort Chipewyan, but it was unable to successfully penetrate the territory controlled by the NWC. As a result, it did not compete seriously with the other company. According to Davidson, the HBC did not appear to have attempted to seriously enter the field of trade in the West, where the NWC already functioned as an independent body (Davidson 1918, 163).[1] As a result, NWC trade was fairly lucrative. HBC returned in 1815 to try to break the NWC monopoly, so that the "two companies vied for Mikisew's loyalty until 1821 when they amalgamated as the Hudson's Bay Company" (Selin 1999, 10). At this point, Fort Chipewyan became the HBC headquarters for the entire region. This merger ended conflict in the area and led to five decades of peaceful monopoly in the region. This stability was disrupted only once, in 1869, when Canada purchased HBC rights to the territories, again opening the fur trade to competition, which led to an influx of free-traders.

In the post-1870 era, an influx of white trappers contributed to the decline of resources, and First Nations people were forced to compete for increasingly scarce resources (Tough 1996, 261). The threat to the renewable resource base was significant, because the Cree relied on trapping revenue for purchasing staple foods and the manufactured implements that had become essential to hunting, fishing, and trapping. Although the Native economy had already partially shifted from hunting for consumption to hunting for trading, the former remained the primary mode of subsistence.

The European traders at Fort Chipewyan were the agents of the fur trade because they represented the mercantilist companies based in Britain and Montreal and later in many other southern locations (McCormack 1984, 63). The Cree produced most of the furs for trade, eventually coming to rely on a mixed economy of subsistence living and commercial trapping. Most of the trade and hence most of the competition was between companies using both local traders and Indian hunters as procurers of furs. Ultimately, this contact led to the intensification of Aboriginal-European relations. The influence of the fur trade gradually created much change for the Cree community, including changes in education, language, religion, and land usage.

The role of external markets was central to the fur trade and its influence on the Cree. First Nations market participation must be examined from the understanding that the fur trade was rooted in trade with other countries. This form of capitalism – mercantilism – was a system of political economy par excellence, "striving after political power through economic means" (Hoogvelt 1997, 3). Because of international competition, the mercantile system required government policies that fostered economic growth and raised revenue. These policies meant that the economy would serve the interests of the polity. The fur trade transferred political control as well as wealth from the colony to the colonizer. This meant that external markets and mercantilist policies shaped post–fur trade Cree-market relations and the Cree's participation in it.

Prior to the fur trade and for a while afterward, the primary unit of production and consumption of the Cree people remained largely intact. Though their participation in the fur trade was vital, the First Nations people remained primarily dependent on the bush mode of production and its lifestyle, heading to town a few times a year primarily to trade and to obtain basic goods such as flour, sugar, and salt. Over time, increasing contact with settlers, traders, and trading companies eroded their traditional economies. The Cree and other Aboriginal groups of the Athabasca region became commercial trappers, dependent on imported European goods.

Decline of the Fur Trade

The fur trade drove the economy of the Athabasca region well into the early part of the 1900s. In the first half of the century, fur prices and fur resources remained high, making fur the dominant commodity. By mid-century, the regional fur trade had lost most of its momentum. One cause was intrusion by the federal government, which increased regulation and restrictions on hunting and trapping. In addition, the creation of Wood Buffalo National Park (WBNP) in 1922 changed the lives of MCFN because it meant that they were required to obtain permits to hunt and trap in the park, even though they had lived, hunted, fished, and gathered berries there since the early 1700s. This increased regulation led to change. Over time, it became increasingly difficult for the Cree to live exclusively from the land. Anthropologist McCormack explains that after 1918, "when game and animal populations declined, Native access to game animals was restricted by legislation and regulations and Native needs for material goods increased [such that] they would turn increasingly to wage labour for their livelihood" (McCormack 1984, 74). Beginning in the 1920s and especially after the 1940s, the Cree were forced to seek wage-earning jobs. Thus, intrusion of the federal government into the market-Cree relationship in the post–fur trade era transformed the means of production and the economic activities of First Nations people.

A second contributing factor to the decline of the fur trade was the activation of another resource sector. Drilling for oil began in 1912 and led to a small economic boom. Even though it was short-lived, it represented the beginning of an important shift in the economy, from fur to oil, that would ultimately transform the focus of resource development in the region. By 1925, industrial capitalism had made its way north via the Northern Alberta Railway, which made it easier to transport other resources, such as salt deposits. In 1964, the Great Canadian Oil Sands (now Suncor Inc.) started construction of its first plant north of the town of Fort McMurray, to transform raw bitumen into usable crude oil. By 1974, ground was broken for the second oil sand plant, Syncrude Canada; and the ensuing oil development once again sparked a flurry of economic development activity in the region.

In addition, the rise of animal rights movements, together with the anti-fur lobby groups and the subsequent global decline in demand for fur products, contributed to the end to the fur industry of the region. By the early 1970s, the community that had served for nearly two hundred years as the headquarters for the regional fur industry was forced to seek out alternative economic activities and pursuits.

From Fur to Oil in the Postwar Era

After the Second World War, capitalist projects in northern Canada developed in relation to important global economic changes. The war effort had stimulated both the American and Canadian economies and their economic integration. Canada found in the United States an important market for the exportation of its vast mineral resources. As a result, the Canadian state started focusing on the development of these resources, most of which were located in the geographic North, where First Nations people represented the bulk of the population.

The postwar focus on developing resources in the North stood in stark contrast to prewar policy. Prewar lack of interest in northern development was, in large part, due to the remoteness of the North, which isolated it from the rest of the nation and the rest of the world. But the discovery of mineral deposits made the North important for meeting the needs and demands of foreign markets. In other words, global demand for resources drew First Nations into the economic agendas of a web of governments, industries, and world markets. Wonders (1971) elaborates: "The increasing attention paid to the North in the postwar years [was] largely the result of the unprecedented demand still swelling for raw materials elsewhere" (5). The growing global demands for oil spurred increased exploration and development activity in the North.

Though the potential of northern Alberta's oil sand development had long been anticipated, it only became feasible when the economics of crude oil supply combined with new technology. In 1941, with the Japanese threatening the Pacific coast, the federal government was alarmed at fuel oil supplies in the West and began to investigate the oil sands as a war emergency project. Thus, this first extraction phase of resource development initially depended on government sponsorship. Although the emergency eventually subsided, the federal government remained involved in oil sand exploration, given its obvious potential use and market value.[2]

Northern Development and MCFN Market Participation

By the early 1970s, postwar capitalist development in the Athabasca region was dominated by oil companies working with the oil sands.[3] For years, however, there was great speculation whether there was a future in the oil sands industry, especially as market fluctuations in the 1970s threatened the profitability of such a venture. As a result, initial development and exploration relied on federal and provincial government support. Syncrude officials concede that they probably would not have got a start if it had not been for the interventions of the provincial and federal governments: "There were doubters, and it was risky in the early days. So [investors] pulled out, and the government of Alberta and Canada bought an interest in Syncrude. And you know, not that that influenced the way we operated the company, but I think it made for an appreciation among the Syncrude folks of how large this whole entity was and what impact it had on the Canadian economy" (Interview with Syncrude representative 2000b).[4] As part of the conditions for government assistance, Syncrude signed an agreement with the federal and provincial governments that required it to assist Aboriginal people in finding work within the oil sands operation. This condition was a critical part of the federal and provincial northern development strategy that sought to create job opportunities for indigenous peoples. However, in his analysis of Syncrude and the politics of oil development, Pratt (1976) argued that Aboriginal people in the region had little reason to be optimistic, since 90 percent were undereducated, unemployed, and forced to live in abominable housing. Hence, he claimed they had little reason to be excited about tar sands development, since they had scant hope of deriving much benefit from Syncrude and succeeding projects (114).

From the outset, Syncrude claims to have recognized that First Nations people had a natural stake in the company's success and decided that it would have to help them transcend the challenges of living and working in a modern industrial society. In the beginning, this required the institutional support of Syncrude's Native Development Program, which was established in 1974. Syncrude's NDP was assigned the task of establishing an action plan for Syncrude-First Nations relations. It tackled issues such as First Nations relocation assistance, housing, education levels, target goals for employment, support services, and cultural awareness programs for supervisors. It was designed to help First Nations employees cope with the transition into Syncrude's culture, while helping Syncrude supervisors better understand and appreciate the different cultural backgrounds of First Nations employees. But one Syncrude official explained that "at the end of the day, hardly any of the people from around here were involved" (Interview with Syncrude representative 2000a). Even when First Nations people were hired, he explained, "they didn't last long [as it was] just too much of a jump from a traditional way of life to working at a big company" (ibid.). Despite its claim of best efforts, the failure of Syncrude to engage and employ First Nations people also meant that the government strategy failed. It failed in part because the arrival of Syncrude created a culture shock within the local First Nations communities. Although First Nations people had participated previously in the fur trade, the new resource development project of the oil sands proved to be substantially different. For the most part, First Nations people were unfamiliar with the ways of modern business and development. They were unaccustomed to forming companies and to bidding on contracts. As a result, the oil sands development created a lot of apprehension, instead of providing a basis for new economic activity.

Eventually, in 1982, Syncrude's Native Affairs Department was dismantled in an effort to incorporate First Nations issues into the normal course of doing business. It was replaced by the First Nations Development Steering Committee, charged with the task of ensuring that Syncrude's commitments to First Nations development were met. For example, Syncrude's post-1982 initiatives included hiring local people to develop training programs and assist in entrepreneurial ventures. As a company, it recognized some of the impediments to fuller participation faced by local First Nations people and devised ways in which it could assist them. To that end, Syncrude developed a program to recruit local First Nations people for specific apprenticeship and management development programs, and provided scholarship programs to assist local First Nations students achieve the higher education required to compete effectively for jobs. The result of their efforts was an increase in the First Nations proportion of the workforce to approximately 5-6 percent by 1985, according to Syncrude officials. Yet Syncrude did not at that point come close to attaining its goal of proportional representation of First Nations people, estimated at 13 percent, which it attained in 1997 (Interview with Syncrude representative 2000b).

From the beginning of its operations, Syncrude recognized the significant impact development and production would have on First Nations people in the region and the importance of proactive steps to include First Nations people in the development process. Hence, it focused its efforts on securing the support of the First Nations population. But government actions also contributed to making corporate-First Nations relations a pressing issue. Linking national economic development to northern resource development, the government sought to connect the local need for jobs with industry's need for a labour force. It was necessary to phase out the belief that First Nations people "could return to trapping, fishing, and hunting or draw upon Indian Affairs relief" (Tough 1996, 307). With environmental change taking its toll in the region, the option of pursuing trapping, fishing, and hunting was less realistic. Eventually, as the traditional economic way of life disappeared and many were unable to make a smooth transition to the wage-labour economy, the onus fell upon the state, through various social assistance programs, to ensure that the economic needs of MCFN members were met.

Dependency and MCFN

Unfortunately, the expansion of the Canadian state and business interests into the Fort Chipewyan region was damaging to the traditional economy of First Nations peoples. Increasingly alienated from their land and from the resource base on which their subsistence way of life had been predicated, MCFN members were no longer able to support themselves economically, and fur-era "colonialism, which involved economic exploitation with occasional rations to sustain the workforce [gave] way to welfare colonialism in which cash assistance" became the new staple commodity (Moscovitch and Webster 1995, 231). The active economic participation that had characterized the fur trade era was replaced by decades of welfare dependence.

The lack of First Nations economic participation in the postwar economy led to a disproportionate reliance on the state. In 1951, the federal government began to include First Nations people in its social assistance programs, beginning with old age pensions. By 1957, these pensions provided close to $40 monthly (which doubled most Canadian household incomes) and offset First Nations financial hardships. Over time, government assistance became a crucial mechanism of economic support for MCFN and the basis of First Nations dependency on the state.

External events and challenges determined the development, or lack thereof, of MCFN during the postwar era. The construction of the W.A.C. Bennett Dam, built in northern British Columbia near the town of Hudson Hope in 1968 by BC Hydro, is a case in point because the community asserted that it severely affected water levels in the Peace-Athabasca Delta of northern Alberta, leading to a chain reaction on the entire ecosystem that devastated traditional fishing and trapping practices. With their traditional ways of life deteriorating, the majority of MCFN members, who engaged in traditional occupations of trapping and fishing for only part of the year, came to depend on social assistance as a way of life.

But conflict soon erupted over the responsibility for the delivery of social support, which became the source of numerous intergovernmental disputes. The federal government claimed that First Nations welfare was within the provincial constitutional sphere of jurisdiction, whereas the provinces maintained that it was a federal responsibility, based on its treaty obligations and fiduciary responsibilities. In general, First Nations people maintained that it was a federal responsibility, highlighting the primacy of their relationship with the federal government, especially given their treaty relationship. They also saw the federal government as an "instrument in promoting capitalist development by pragmatic intervention where market forces fail or remain absent" (Abele 1987, 311). In the end, these responsibilities fell to the federal government; as social welfare services increased the federal presence in the North, it eventually led to the extension of full-scale colonial administration (ibid.).

Globalization and the Alberta Oil Industry

In the postwar era, government development initiatives assisted the marketplace. Increased global economic pressures changed government roles and market expectations to adapt to an integrated world economy. The state transformed from directing national development to providing an environment for unfettered economic growth. This transformation manifested itself in the dismantling of regulations and restrictions that previously inhibited the free flow of goods and hampered international trade. To be viewed as competitive, states focused on providing stable and attractive investment environments. Part of this strategy required the devolution of control and the dismantling of barriers impeding economic growth, wealth generation, and market participation.

With the looming depletion of global oil sources, the Canadian economy, primarily in the traditional hinterland, once again focused on strong resource-based companies able to compete internationally and meet global needs, especially in the energy sector. Greg Stringham of the Canadian Association of Petroleum Producers (CAPP) predicted that oil sands development would "have a significant role to play not only in the Canadian economy, but in the world economy" (CBC 2002d). Globalization is most evident in the mineral sector in the North, where technology is capital-intensive and a small number of large companies are dominant. The Athabasca oil sands development is also dependent on technology. According to Stringham, "It used to be that we would only recover about 15 to 20 percent of the conventional reserve and the rest of it would just stay in the ground because it was too hard to get out. New technologies are going after that remaining 75-80 percent that's in the ground" (ibid.). Industry analysts claim that the oil sands contain 300 billion barrels of oil, as much as Saudi Arabia, the world's largest petroleum power. If all that oil were recoverable, the oil sands could satisfy world demand for a decade, but there is an important distinction to be made. Oil in Saudi Arabia "is producible probably somewhere around a dollar a barrel. In the tar sands you're looking at somewhere around $20 a barrel" (ibid.). Although new technology has since reduced that cost to approximately $12 a barrel, Canadian producers still pay more to produce oil than most of their competitors. The higher the price of oil, the more the extraction of tar sands oil becomes viable and profitable. Thus, the development of Alberta oil remains largely dependent on fluctuations in global markets and global demands.

TLE and MCFN-Market Participation

Though global demand for finite resources generally requires state retrenchment, there is still a role for the government to play in Canadian economic development. For instance, neoliberal governments must create a climate conducive to investment. At the same time, they must make a collaborative and co-operative effort to improve the effectiveness of regulations governing nonrenewable resource development. The primary economic task of federal and provincial governments is to create and sustain an appropriate economic environment, to provide regulations, and to make strategic decisions about the overall direction development should take. Although both globalization and neoliberalism press for smaller, less active government, the Canadian government remains active in First Nations economic development because of its legal and constitutional obligations. This means that both levels of government have a role in transforming a First Nation's economic activity. As one provincial official explained, the province wants to ensure that First Nations people "are part of the industrial development that is going on" (Interview with provincial government representative 2000b). For this reason, the federal government wanted to ensure that members of Treaty 8 were involved in the latest phase of economic development. Improving the situation of First Nations communities and individuals is a neoliberal priority, since it focuses on strengthening First Nations participation in the economy. As former INAC minister Robert Nault once declared, "It's my role to participate in helping to create an economy, or giving the people the opportunity to look at particular avenues to create an economy" (CBC 2001). Justifying government's attention to First Nations economic development, one federal government representative insisted, "I don't think that is so much a government agenda but a reality in the world today. I think that is part of globalization" (Interview with federal government representative 2000d).

A significant component of government involvement in First Nations economies is financial, since lack of capital is a primary constraint to economic self-determination and the development of capital opportunities. The federal government must dismantle institutions that impede economic activity and provide the financial means for self-sufficiency. In order to optimize its investments in First Nations people, governments need to have an ongoing commitment to the process. Governments thus play an important part in fostering a more supportive environment and providing access to economic and financial tools for increased economic participation.

MCFN settled the TLE in 1986 on the assumption that "land, resource and financial arrangements provide for an influx of dollars and other economic development measures into First Nations communities [that] increase their financial and economic development prospects" (Working Group on First Nations Participation in the Economy 2001, 13). Increased capital meant increased decision-making power, as bands and band members ultimately decided how to allocate that capital.[5] Accordingly, MCFN also worked toward building a lucrative relationship with the oil industry, most notably with major producers in the area, such as Syncrude. Although its focus remained steadfast on the outstanding terms of the treaty, it was clearly looking ahead to a new phase of economic participation.

Post-TLE Economic Development
The success of the MCFN vision lies in the community's ability to develop and diversify an economic base that will enable it to compete in the marketplace, and by extension, improve the quality of life for its members. To that end, MCFN strives to generate economic growth that will enable it to confront social challenges. New avenues for economic development are necessary because, as Waquan (1992) conceded, "the sad reality of it all is everything has been affected with no hope of recovering or healing" (17). There is a sense that it is impossible for MCFN members to live as they did years ago "because there has been too much development and globalization" (Interview with MCFN member 2000q). Despite what some might consider a sudden leap into the modern world, members of MCFN assert that they have neither forfeited nor forgotten their legacy as stewards of the land. Their indigenous identity is not lost in the pragmatic recognition that it is impossible to recapture or live exclusively by traditional means. Instead, economic development strategies encompass First Nations values while also recognizing the importance of being able to compete and participate in the globalized economy. The key to balancing these two elements lies in their choice of activity.

Waquan suggested that "we must continue to focus our energies on economic and human resource development [because] these two areas are often seen as separate but they are, in fact, very related" (Selin 1999, 6). Because limited development opportunities exist within the community itself, MCFN has developed important employment and training opportunities for its members by developing the community. First, MCFN and the Alberta Treasury Branch entered into partnership to open a branch in Fort

Chipewyan in May 2002 to deal with the lack of reliable banking services in Fort Chipewyan. It is located in the centre of town and is accessible to everyone in the community. This institution offers a full range of banking services as well as a cash machine and provides employment for two MCFN members. Second, the band purchased land in Fort McMurray with TLE monies to build a Super 8 Motel; MCFN owns 62.5 percent of the shares (Mikisew Cree First Nation 2002d, 1).[6] The point of these projects was to ensure that MCFN received an excellent return on its investment when profits were shared between the partners. They also acted as good examples of revenue generation. As part of the expansion project, MCFN has reached an agreement to create a special hotel management training program for two of its members. If the pilot project works out, the plan will be expanded to recruit two more members. Finally, in Edmonton, MCFN purchased a new business that opened in July 2002, manufacturing lifting and safety products such as slings, safety harnesses, and Canadian Standards Association–approved rope. The business aims to provide employment for ten to fifteen band members living in Edmonton (DIAND 2004b).

By virtue of its many economic initiatives, MCFN is the largest single employer in the community. It employs 103 people in its government, business, and education departments. Hence, for the band, economic development means employment for its members. But this job-creation function merely offsets the deterioration of other employment sectors within the community. Previously, a large number of the jobs available in Fort Chipewyan had been in the public sector. Nine government agencies with offices in the community (three federal and six provincial) once provided fifty-eight permanent positions (deCardinale 1996, c-7). But with the cutbacks in agencies and departments across government, fewer jobs are available in the community in this sector. For instance, one member pointed out how there used to be jobs with Parks Canada; but with government cutbacks, "those jobs aren't there that used to be" (Interview with MCFN member 2000h).

Profit-generating ventures are another integral element of the MCFN development program because profits can be reinvested in the general operation of the First Nation. The point of this arrangement was initially to assist MCFN in developing the Allison Bay Reserve, transforming it into the centre of the MCFN community. Through revenues and services generated by its various band-owned businesses, MCFN committed a total of $15 million over eight years (1996-2004) to the Allison Bay Reserve project (DIAND 1996b). Yet profit is not the sole impetus for economic development. MCFN member Ed Courtoreille, former president of 2000 Plus (an MCFN business now operating under the umbrella of MESG), responded to questions about what motivates him: "It's not the profits that we are gaining for our First Nation. It's seeing the positive changes that occur within our people as they pursue a better way of life which comes from steady employment, financial success, independence, and increased self-esteem" (Selin 1999, 5). This suggests that as part of its economic development strategy, MCFN is committed to improving the welfare of its people with success not measured simply in jobs and income but in human and cultural terms.

Of course, another way for MCFN to generate revenue is to tax its own people. Taxation is an important globalization issue because it raises questions about the financing of self-government. Already MCFN leaders have expressed an interest in taxing its members. As one member explained, "Self-government is the day we have our own taxation" (Interview with MCFN member 2000h). This view is shared by the province, which maintains that self-government means paying your own way. Clearly, a dynamic economic base is necessary to provide the means for self-government, but many MCFN members fail to make this connection: "It [self-government] is not explained well enough to the people," one member explained. "They say that it is good, but in the long run we will have to start taxing them, tax them on their lot" (ibid.). For some MCFN members, if self-government means the end of their treaty right to non-taxation, then it is not a good idea.[7] Given the anti-taxation sentiment held by many First Nations people, MCFN leaders admit that imposing taxation on band members would be a "hard sell," because many members do not understand the tax system and do not support the notion of paying taxes. Yet MCFN leaders see taxation as inevitable if they are to sustain their political and economic operations. As one member noted, "We are not sitting on oil or anything, [so taxation] would be the first thing to figure out [for deciding] how we are going to make money to survive" (Interview with MCFN member 2000i). MCFN has taken a first step by taxing on-reserve businesses.[8] Although MCFN has a substantial capital base from which to fund a large proportion of its programs, the question of taxation for additional revenue is integral to the issue of self-government. Hence, taxation remains one element of self-sufficiency that it will have to tackle in the future.

Resource-Based Economic Development

Immediately following the TLE, MCFN participation in the local resource-based economy was still weak. Although a $20 billion resource development project was occurring immediately to the south in the oil sands, MCFN did not appear to be benefiting. Yet the oil patch was supposed to provide opportunity for MCFN and other local First Nations, not only in direct employment but also in contract opportunities. MCFN viewed participation in oil sands activities as a way to optimize its economic potential. Reaching out to the private sector was an important part of its economic strategy. It was also important to Syncrude, which viewed First Nations people as an important reserve of labour – "an untapped source of human resource" (Interview with Syncrude representative 2000b).

After the TLE, the time was ripe for tapping that source. Syncrude set out to assist MCFN in developing new businesses in areas that remained undeveloped, to carve out a niche for MCFN in the oil sands market. Syncrude led the way, working with MCFN to establish businesses, then opening up contracting opportunities for local First Nations business and working with them to enhance their competitive capacity. It helped MCFN launch 2000 Plus in 1991, a labour contracting company supplying both skilled and semi-skilled tradesmen and labourers, along with equipment, for major oil sands companies in the area. The over-riding goal was simple: to create employment for band members. It started in 1991 with just eight employees and has grown to a workforce of 120. It is currently developing a trained work force composed mainly of MCFN members living in Fort McMurray, whose employment numbers jump to 220 during the regularly scheduled shutdowns for maintenance of machinery at the plants. This makes 2000 Plus the third-largest employer of First Nations people in the region, after Syncrude and Suncor (Selin 1999, 4).[9] In 1997, 2000 Plus signed a five-year contract with Syncrude, and one year later, it signed a contract for the same length of time with Suncor, followed by an agreement to provide maintenance and labour services to Shell Canada for a period of eighteen months. Syncrude therefore helped MCFN overcome some of the barriers that previously impeded its economic participation.

In addition, the presence of external work opportunities increased MCFN economic participation in the post-TLE era. First Nations businesses, such as 2000 Plus, which initially received assistance from Syncrude, achieved recognition for their success through national awards, and then expanded to work with a variety of oil and gas companies in the region. Eventually, economic and political links to the regional community improved MCFN's ability to access broader markets for its products and services and developed its labour expertise.

But Syncrude helped not only MCFN as a band but also individual MCFN members to compete more effectively in the marketplace. For example, with the support of Syncrude, MCFN member David Tuccaro purchased Neegan Development (an MCFN contract company) from the band to run it himself.[10] To assist Tuccaro in making the business a success, Syncrude financial managers assessed the company to identify areas where Tuccaro could concentrate his efforts. For instance, they noted that the business was losing income maintaining older equipment that was in need of replacement. Syncrude sent in a mobile maintenance crew to work with Tuccaro and set up maintenance systems that helped Neegan Development replace equipment. That, one Syncrude official remarked, "essentially got things off the ground, and Dave went on to build Neegan into a profitable and reputable company" (Interview with Syncrude representative 2000b).

Tuccaro, who is now based in Calgary, owns and controls several businesses, including Tuccaro Inc., which finances property rentals and commercial development; First Nations Global Investments (a money market investment firm); First Nations Technical Services (environmental engineering and laboratory services); Tuc's Contracting (water and vacuum truck services); and CreeAtive Custom Woodworking (a furniture-manufacturing company in Calgary). In speaking about his success, Tuccaro explains that First Nations people "have to start saying we can do it ourselves, or someone else will still be looking after us ... I left my community because there wasn't enough opportunity for me there. I had to compete in the Canadian [and now global] marketplace" (Black 1999, 3). As Tuccaro seeks more ways to expand his businesses, he actively promotes global business opportunities for the world's indigenous peoples (National Aboriginal Achievement Foundation 1999).

Tuccaro's success indicates the extent to which individual Mikisew Cree members are able to participate in the local, national, and global marketplace. Corporate assistance has proven invaluable for struggling individuals keen on ending their dependence. As one Syncrude official observed, "What I have always found is that most of the First Nations people just need some encouragement and some opportunity. They just need a light at the end of the tunnel and some mentoring ... once they have that opportunity I can tell you they are no different than anybody else. They are just going to get at it and do it" (Interview with Syncrude representative 2000b).

With First Nations populations growing, oil sands producers recognize that good working relations with First Nations are conducive to maintaining a labour pool and maximizing shareholder value in the long run. The contemporary view of the corporate-First Nation relationship is that it is a significant investment, yielding a large return. Only twenty years ago, First Nation leaders were largely ignored by the corporate executives; today, there is an important and familiar relationship between the two groups. As one official made clear, "You make sure the First Nations people in the region – and particularly for us here, because there are a high percentage of them – are onside with what you are doing, and you are going to maximize shareholder value at the end of the day" (ibid.).

At the same time, the tar sands industries must compete in the global market for the investment capital required for ongoing non-renewable-resource development. Globalization thus presents tar sands companies with an extremely intense challenge. They must do everything they can to be competitive, and this includes having good relations with their neighbours. In the present investment environment, the litmus test for industry-First Nations relations lies in the regulatory process. The better the relations with the local First Nations people, the better the chances are of avoiding a costly hearing on the development of new sites. Because a hearing costs $4 million or $5 million, "having bad relations with local First Nations people in this area would just be a nightmare [because] you don't want the expense [of a hearing]. But the expense of the hearing is not the thing. The expense of the delay of approval

– that is the thing" (Interview with Syncrude representative 2000a). As oil sand companies seek to increase profits, they seek to increase production, preferably unencumbered by hearings and protests. Consequently, the corporate approach has been to develop long-term relationships with First Nations so that they can deal with any grievances on an ongoing basis. For example, in its effort to develop a new site (known in the region as the Suncor Millennium Project), Suncor received approval without any interventions by local First Nations. This meant that public hearings proceeded *pro forma*. According to one spokesperson, this is testament to Suncor's relationship and demonstrates the value of doing consultations on an ongoing basis (Interview with Suncor representative 2000).

Part of the allure of a good MCFN-industry relationship is the potential employment opportunities generated by the oil sands companies. The majority of employment prospects, however, remain in labour-oriented jobs, such as waste disposal, pest control, roadwork, and environmental cleanup. As a result, MCFN is concerned not only with the number of jobs created, but increasingly with the kinds of jobs created and the limits of its involvement in resource development in the region. Although its relationship with the oil sands companies has clearly generated jobs, jobs are not sufficient. Many MCFN members do not believe that the corporations are doing enough. Others simply observe that "they don't benefit Mikisew" (Interview with MCFN member 2000g). As one member pointed out, "When you think of these companies, they always try to get you in there to do labour work. They never ever offer to give you a percentage of the company, like we are only good enough to do labour. And we don't like that. We want to be part of that company, which means we want a percentage of it so we can buy into what they are starting" (ibid.). MCFN's desire for more meaningful participation in the development process is inhibited only by the fact that MCFN does not possess the money required to proceed to the partnership level (namely, as part owner), despite its aspiration to participate more equitably in the oil industry.[11] To transform this situation, MCFN is developing the political and economic strength required to participate in development projects at a more substantial level, and it is suing for control of Alberta's oil sands and for compensation for past revenue. Beginning in 1996, MCFN launched legal action accusing the federal government of defrauding it of mineral title. MCFN lawyer Jeff Rath argues that the federal government was aware of the great mineral deposits and potential wealth at the signing of Treaty 8 and failed to release this information to MCFN. Furthermore, he maintains, Ottawa and the province dissuaded MCFN from claiming oil sands lands during its TLE negotiations. Hence, MCFN is pursuing legal action as part of its strategy to benefit more fully from local resource development.[12]

Another part of MCFN's economic development strategy involves working through the Athabasca Tribal Council (ATC). Located in Fort McMurray,

ATC represents a conglomerate of Treaty 8 First Nations that includes the Athabasca Chipewyan First Nation, Mikisew Cree First Nation, Chipewyan Prairie First Nation, Fort McMurray #468 First Nation, and Fort McKay First Nation. ATC works effectively with the local communities as an advocate and a resource. While ATC provides social services (education, training, and social welfare support), MCFN has been particularly interested in its industry relations initiatives. In 1999, ATC negotiated the first in a series of tripartite agreements with local industry, the provincial government, and its member nations to address socioeconomic conditions and target life skill issues that continue to plague local First Nations.

The initial deal, known as the ATC/Industry Capacity Building Agreement, signed in March 1999, had three purposes. First, it ensured that industry worked with ATC and member First Nations to develop community capacity. Second, it identified community and regional issues and opportunities to resolve those issues pertaining to industrial development. Third, industry worked with ATC to develop strategies to obtain government support for addressing outstanding First Nations issues. In general, the agreement focused on five areas where capacity building was required: the capacity for environmental consultation; education; employment and training initiatives; human infrastructure (health and social welfare); physical infrastructure; and further long-term benefits extending beyond the period of resource extraction. Negotiated by Marlene Poitras, former CEO of ATC and a member of MCFN, this deal consolidated institutional support for capacity building and represented long-term strategic planning for First Nations participation in regional operations. As one government representative put it, "This time, the First Nations of northeastern Alberta get their own chance, as it were, to tap a gusher" (DIAND 2003a). With industry and government responsibilities identified and their associated financial support confirmed, ATC has provided an important institutional base that has supported MCFN economic development ambitions. ATC also plays a key role in accessing funding support and coordinating government, industry, and First Nations initiatives.

Social Problems and Social Enhancement

Despite MCFN's ambitions and successes, social problems continue to plague the MCFN community. MCFN leaders recognize that efforts to improve the lives of their members are complicated by the bitter legacy of residential schools, lack of education, and lack of life skills. This means that membership development requires many changes that include ending membership dependency on the state. With many social and economic hurdles to overcome, dependence on social welfare transfer payments remains endemic. They are a major source of income in the community. The community is trying to transform this situation through a unique and innovative MCFN program called Social Enhancement.

The mandate of the Social Enhancement program is to achieve social reform. The program's goal is to motivate and encourage individuals to exercise their self-determination to build self-reliance and to end their dependency on welfare. As part of the social development endeavour, Social Enhancement teaches people that welfare is not a right and that government will not always be there to take care of them. Instead, it instructs them to seek out other economic alternatives. One Social Enhancement officer suggests, "Welfare is not a right, so we have to change our way of thinking" (Interview with MCFN member 2000h). Another echoes that idea, saying "I think a lot of it, too, is trying to get them in the right frame of mind, trying to get them thinking long term, and trying to them to look long term, accessing or working towards their goal (Interview with MCFN member 2000j). To that end, the Social Enhancement program also encourages education, because there appears to be a direct correlation between lack of education and high levels of welfare dependence. Education is an important, if somewhat obvious, target, given the low numbers of high school graduates: "There is a lot of opportunity out there for employment. In terms of the community, there are not enough people; people don't have enough training or education to get those jobs. [There is] low education and low training" (Interview with MCFN member 2000j). With current rates of high school completion hovering somewhere between 10 percent and 30 percent, education is an important component of social reform (deCardinale 1996, 9).

In accounting for the low educational levels, one member suggests that "it's a combination of everything. I think it's the combination that could be the school system, it could be the lack of support at home, it could be low self-esteem, low confidence, it could be a social problem. It could be drugs or alcohol [or] family abuse" (ibid.). Hence, a significant part of the social reform project consists of the difficult task of motivating people to return to school and assisting them in overcoming impediments that function as barriers to educational accomplishment. For those without educational ambitions, Social Enhancement also works to provide them with alternatives to welfare. For the most part, however, alternative approaches to welfare focus primarily on economic and social development. This means that the Social Enhancement office works in conjunction with another agency, Employment Services, to provide members with basic life skills and job-related training. This agency serves members in a variety of ways: helping them to prepare resumés, apply for funding, and apply for jobs; assisting members who are involved in apprenticeship programs; and working with members on setting goals and setting out the steps required to achieve those goals – all of which are designed to end welfare dependence.

The federal government is involved in welfare reform because welfare reform is a critical component of the neoliberal agenda. Federal involvement provides training and skills development opportunities geared to enhance both individual abilities and meet market needs. In effect, MCFN works in collaboration with Human Resources Development Canada to develop links with local employers as part of its social reform program. This is intended to provide welfare recipients with employment skills while also providing local companies with much-needed labour. In the spring of 1999, through one such initiative, Syncrude hired forty-seven community members to work at a scheduled maintenance shutdown. But what happened, as one member puts it, was that "our people weren't ready, and after their first cheque a lot of them were either terminated or they quit" (Interview with MCFN member 2000h). Although the rate of attrition suggests that Social Enhancement, as a program, is not working, this member added, "But then I look at the thirteen people that went through it and finished and completed it and then I think it was worth it" (ibid.). Evidence of the program's success is reflected in the success of those who made the transition from welfare to work. Because the majority of those who start the program do not last even a month, one member suggests that employment is just a "band-aid solution" (Interview with MCFN member 2000j). Nevertheless, full employment remains a central priority for MCFN. Although it is not obvious how successful this program will be in eradicating MCFN welfare dependence, what is clear is that federal and provincial governments are eager to work with First Nations communities and the private sector to enhance employment opportunities for First Nations people. What is also clear is that MCFN appears eager to eliminate welfare dependence through Social Enhancement-type programs.

The MCFN Social Enhancement program not only provides employment opportunities and welfare alternatives but also makes available basic assistance to twenty-eight families and forty-six single people. The program pays for such items as utilities (twenty-eight families/persons) and rent (nine families/persons). In addition, the program provides bereavement assistance to families and individuals in need. A large operation, Social Enhancement had a total monthly expenditure in February 2002 of over $50,000 (Mikisew Cree First Nation 2002a, 13). Social spending represents a significant expense, but it remains consistent with MCFN values that emphasize community needs and well being. For that reason, MCFN appears willing to spend the money required to help its members acquire the basic necessities and opportunities. Sensitive and understanding of the needs of its members who are socially and economically challenged and at risk, the band is committed and dedicated to improving the circumstances, environment, and future of its people, as its mission statement asserts. For all intents and purposes, its programs seem to be working: poverty no longer appears to be a crippling problem, reflecting an improvement in the socioeconomic status of the community.

As MCFN has aggressively pursued an active economic agenda, it has sought to improve the quality of life of its membership. Part of its strategy has involved developing and diversifying its economic base to meet the needs of the people who depend upon it. In effect, through its subsidies and programs, MCFN has generated wealth and opportunity that enable it to reinvest in the community. Even the importance of self-sufficiency and self-determination does not eclipse the underlying concerns for community needs and well-being that are rooted in local ownership and authority as well as education, training, and career development.

Conclusion

Industry, government, and MCFN share an interest in increasing MCFN's economic participation. Accomplishing this goal requires a collaborative effort. It requires the dismantling of barriers that inhibit First Nations participation in the marketplace. It demands a supportive business climate, government development dollars, training programs, and joint support for individual and community-based capacity building. Finally, it involves access to capital and access to markets.

As MCFN, the state, and industry work to increase MCFN economic participation, they proceed from a set of shared assumptions that are mutually reinforcing. At the core is the assumption that the key to First Nations' self-determination lies in the ability of First Nations to compete effectively and independently in the marketplace. Implicit in this assumption is that equality found in the marketplace will ultimately lead to socioeconomic parity. Economic strategies developed by First Nations organizations, the private sector, and government are therefore designed to achieve practical results – that is, to overcome challenges in First Nations socioeconomic development and to strengthen First Nations participation in the economy.

MCFN economic participation and its socioeconomic status have also grown because MCFN economic participation is not entirely dependent upon state funding or industry initiative. With its own capital base, MCFN possesses sufficient capital to meet important political and social objectives and to take advantage of emerging economic opportunities. This capital base also means that MCFN can pay its own way. Since many First Nations communities and businesses lack equity, they encounter difficulty in acquiring adequate business financing. Access to loan guarantees, equity, and debt financing are important for both business and community development. Hence, a capital base is integral to economic development and self-determination.

In conclusion, the post-TLE experience of MCFN stands in stark contrast to its pre-TLE experience. What is clear is that it has just begun its journey in economic development and participation. As part of this process, the community is concentrating on developing capital, capacity, and training; regaining control of lands and resources; developing new partnerships; educating its workforce; and ultimately increasing its self-determination. Since MCFN remains focused on the future, it could be considered a model for other communities.

6
Transforming First Nations Governance

Just as a series of historical events persuaded, influenced, and shaped Crown-MCFN-market relations in the past, so current events influence modern manifestations of Crown-MCFN-market relations. The transformation of MCFN governance is inextricably linked to changes in state development strategies that facilitate the demands of the global economic order and market demands for finite resources.

Since the state functions as the critical instrument through which globalization's demands are met and mediated, Crown-MCFN-market relations directly correlate to shifts in the international political economy. For instance, in the early colonial phase of Canadian history, when the global economy functioned to seek out and exploit resources, and when the state was largely laissez-faire, First Nations enjoyed a significant degree of political autonomy and unobtrusive market activity. That is, they were not subjects of the state but active participants in the inter-European wars and agents of economic development as key actors in the fur trade. Then, in the postwar era of increased regulation of the global marketplace and the rise of the interventionist state, First Nations autonomy was restricted and their economic activity subverted. The result was the expansion of government powers and, consequently, the transformation of First Nations people into wards of the state. In the present era of globalization, as the neoliberal state promotes unfettered market development, there is a growing movement to restore First Nations independence, political self-government, and economic self-sufficiency. While several factors have influenced current policy changes (e.g., the Hawthorn Report in the 1960s, greater Aboriginal organization in the 1970s, constitutional change in the 1980s, conflicts such as Oka, as well as the Royal Commission on Aboriginal Peoples in the 1990s), there is an important and often overlooked correlation among global economic imperatives, state policy initiatives, and First Nations self-determination. Because capitalism requires stability of the investment environment, the time has come to settle First Nations claims.

How have things changed for First Nations as a result of globalization? As one person observed,

> I have watched for twenty-two years how the community has gotten better and better. I mean, I can tell you when I first went up there it was not unlike a typical First Nations community – broken-down cars in the front yard, the place looked like a mess. Now, you go up there today and people have their houses painted, they have fences, there is a new 4x4 in the driveway, there is a Skidoo in the back of it, and the kids have got designer clothes on – all this stuff that has all come from getting out there and having an opportunity. (Interview with federal government representative 2000a)

Although this is one view of the good society, it also represents a neoliberal vision of success – which raises the question, is this transformation due to globalization? And is this indicative of assimilation? The problem with conflating economic development with assimilation is essentialism. First Nations cultures are not static, and it is impossible to sustain the traditional First Nations way without also changing. At the same time, if the only consequence of self-determination is that it benefits capitalism, then it is regrettable. The key, therefore, is choice: First Nations people deciding how to combine or balance the important elements of traditional life and modern demands. Neoliberal policies create new governing institutions that are conducive to capitalism and that advocate market solutions to social programming. At the same time, globalization provides economic development that enables First Nations people to use capital business ventures to generate revenue to pay for social housing and health care needs. It also enables them to develop important youth and elder programs, healing camps, and other culturally based initiatives. In effect, globalization supports market solutions to social restructuring, primarily through dismantling the Keynesian welfare state. However, this restructuring also gives First Nations the opportunity to construct their own political and economic regimes that meet their own governance needs. This is what makes MCFN self-determination both unique and appealing: it tries to balance the needs of its community with the demands of the world in which it lives.

The Mikisew Model

The experience of the Mikisew Cree First Nation illustrates one possible path toward self-determination. The MCFN experience suggests that certain characteristics are essential for the realization of self-determination. These qualities include external development (i.e., market opportunity and access to financial capital), internal assets (i.e., natural resources, human capital, and institutions of governance and culture), and development strategy (i.e., choice of development activity).

MCFN possesses a high degree of political autonomy and has sufficient resources to develop its economy. It also has highly developed institutions, including formal rules and procedures for decision making, a professional financial and record system, and strong governance institutions (chief executive and capable bureaucracy). It has also made the critical decision to separate electoral politics from the management of business enterprise, an important institutional development. Finally, it has made specific choices regarding the allocation of workers, capital, and resources. MCFN has achieved success in managing three issue areas critical for political and economic development: (1) money; (2) geography; and (3) industry.

Money

Because the federal government is not granting further funding for self-government negotiations, First Nations must now have their own revenues to draw upon. Thus, a capital base is critical for the operationalization and implementation of self-determination. MCFN possesses the necessary capital to do this, and its experience suggests that only with sufficient dollars can self-government occur. For those First Nations that do not have adequate resources, self-government may be elusive, since neoliberalism brings benefits only to those with some leverage in the marketplace. Therefore, self-determination is increasingly predicated on possessing the financial ability to make it happen.

Because much of MCFN's capital base is the result of the treaty land entitlement, a critical part of its success lies not only in the settlement of its claim but also in the financial award that accompanied it. As one member commented, "As a result of [our increased resources], we are in a better position to identify economic opportunities which again at the end of the day will sustain our First Nation in different areas, individually and collectively as a First Nation" (Interview with MCFN member 2000q).

Money alone, however, is not a magical ingredient that increases decision-making power or economic development. By way of evidence, one need only look at Saskatchewan, where the provincial and federal governments signed a TLE agreement with the chiefs of twenty-two First Nations on 22 September 1992. The terms of the Saskatchewan Treaty Land Entitlement Framework Agreement provided $450 million over twelve years to twenty-two bands to purchase land and mineral rights. Each of the bands was required to purchase "reserve" land to a maximum of 1.67 million acres (Saskatchewan 1994, 9). The requirement that the bulk of monies be spent only on land for reserves was the key problem. Land choices were largely agricultural and did not represent a good investment, since agricultural land limits labour force and economic development. Nor did the agreements take into account the inability of the land base to transform socioeconomic problems. As a result, the government of Saskatchewan had to return to the table to work out new models of governance to address socioeconomic disparities. The lesson from Saskatchewan, therefore, is that in order to foster self-determination, cash compensation must come without restrictions on its use.

In general, current federal First Nations policy focuses on self-government; yet few bands possess the capital base necessary to actualize self-government. Money is important not only for social development but also for political development, since the wealthier a First Nation is, the more efficacious its government can be. This is why cash compensation is such a critical element of the TLE process. One federal official acknowledges that "some [First Nations] worked out really well with it – Mikisew being one" (Interview with federal government representative 2000c).

Geography

What about location? Is the relatively remote location of First Nations peoples a factor in their development? According to Mel Watkins, "Large-scale resource projects are said by their proponents to create 'development.' In fact, for native people what has resulted is properly characterized as 'underdevelopment'" (1977, 91). Yet a "typology" of First Nations communities arising out of census statistics concluded that Fort Chipewyan was located in a highly developed region of northern Alberta (Armstrong 1999, 3). This report categorized 491 Aboriginal communities and categorized them as above average, of typical disparity, and of high disparity, based on indicators of socioeconomic well-being that included employment, income, education, and housing, relative to the average Canadian community. A north-south and bicoastal pattern emerged, with above-average communities (characterized by relatively high employment, educational attainment, and individual incomes, as well as lower levels of household crowding) being located in the south.[1] Thus, the identification of one northeastern region of Alberta as above average is significant. Geographic proximity to urban or resource-rich areas may provide advantages to development, since access to resources and integration with urban labour markets may be two pathways to success (ibid., 4). Even communities in typically unfavourable or isolated locations can pursue and take advantage of opportunities that can lead to socioeconomic success.

Although located far from urban centres such as Fort McMurray, Edmonton, and Calgary, Fort Chipewyan's remoteness does not inhibit MCFN self-determination because it is not an impediment to development. One MCFN member suggests that geographic isolation "has been a blessing, because it has forced Fort Chipewyan to be innovative and self-motivating" (Interview with MCFN member 2000q). In addition, proximity to a city can make a First Nations community dependent on municipal provision of services or local business opportunities. In contrast, remoteness has forced MCFN to develop its own opportunities locally, such as teaching people plumbing and building-related skills so that they can build and repair their own houses, instead of flying others up to do the work for them. Geography forces MCFN to be both independent and self-reliant.

Industry

Finally, it is worth identifying the efforts of local companies (such as Syncrude, Suncor, and Alliance Pipeline) to develop a new economic relationship with MCFN. Though Syncrude was originally compelled to work with the local First Nations communities, this compulsion did not diminish its ongoing contributions to MCFN. With Syncrude's assistance, MCFN was able to exploit local entrepreneurial opportunities and get its foot in the door of local resource-development projects. In addition, the company itself set employment targets to ensure that its employment demographics reflected the local population. Certainly, corporate assistance dressed up as social concern ultimately serves corporate interest; yet this proactive corporate approach to working with First Nations is still not the norm among industry. For example, De Beers, which also operates in northern Canada, was unwilling to set targets for hiring northern and First Nations workers at its Snap Lake site. Although regional First Nations groups and government officials pressed the company for a commitment, De Beers' goal was to hire as many northerners as it could, without specifying any hiring targets (CBC 2002c). Yet targets are important for determining what effect resource development will have on the northern economy.

MCFN's success at managing money, geography, and industry does not mean that self-determination can occur only within this particular framework and with these specific components. Self-determination is progressing in other communities with other characteristics. Ultimately, MCFN offers a model for self-determination and shows why it matters. It also suggests that state retrenchment and capitalist development both help and hinder self-determination, as some communities flourish under neoliberalism while others flounder.

Globalization and First Nations Governance

Is self-determination a step forward for First Nations if they are beings pressured into land claims only to open up their lands to resource development? Is it a choice if it threatens to destroy those fundamental elements which make First Nations people Aboriginal? Often self-determination is framed as a choice between progressive development (assimilation) and stagnant traditionalism (fossilization). Most often, this dilemma unfolds in northern Canada, where non-renewable-resource extraction dominates the economic landscape and where the freedoms associated with self-determination are framed in terms of resource development.

As some First Nations embrace self-determination based on resource development, the issue of choice may lead to polarization within communities.

Already a new group of First Nations is emerging, one that competes more vigorously in the marketplace than others. Differences once found only between individual members can now also be found between different communities, as different models of self-determination lead to different types of First Nations. In essence, issues of self-determination increasingly raise issues of unequal relations between First Nations. Market-driven self-determination may lead to the separation of First Nations into "have" and "have not" groups.[2] Thus, state retrenchment and market participation leads not only to development but also to different types or levels of development, which ultimately creates a new distinction between First Nations groups. These changes raise new concerns about the potential effects of land claims settlement and resource development on First Nations.[3]

The experience of the Mikisew Cree First Nation introduces new ways of thinking about the globalization–First Nation relationship. Neoliberalism provides a policy environment that privileges the marketplace and disproportionately benefits the wealthy; but it also works to the benefit of well-resourced First Nations. Therefore, in the neoliberal era, it is possible to construct a type of self-determination based on First Nations participation in the marketplace. Of course, an unfortunate consequence of globalization may be that self-determination is measured in terms of economic success. Regardless, neoliberalism and self-determination are linked; and because neoliberalism is closely wedded to globalization, globalization and First Nations are linked. Conceptions of globalization and governance therefore provide a framework through which we can better understand and explain the nature of changes occurring in the state–First Nations relationship, as well as those occurring *within* many First Nations communities.

Notes

Introduction

1 The term "First Nations" is "used by many status Indian communities, and by the Assembly of First Nations, to refer to either Indian Act bands, or the historic, political and cultural entities that are now fragmented into bands by federal legislation" (Green 2001, 716). This definition is useful because it suggests that the term "First Nations" is a term developed by Indians to define themselves as nations as opposed to government-created bands. "First Nations" is a term that has become most associated with the goal of self-government and/or self-determination.

2 As Janine Brodie (1997a) explains, in the new global order, the neoliberal orthodoxy puts the same demands on all governments, both national and sub-national: that they eliminate their debts, stop regulating business, sell their assets to the private sector, and dismantle the welfare state all in order to be more competitive in the international market (223-24).

3 For more on this line of thought, see Angus 1990.

Chapter 1: Meeting Mikisew

1 Air Mikisew, an MCFN business venture, operates two flights daily between Fort Chipewyan and Fort McMurray, flying 15,000 passengers yearly. The airline also carries 3,000 Syncrude employees between Fort Chipewyan, Fort McMurray, and Edmonton annually, provides air service for major tourist operations, and provides emergency medical evacuation services. In addition, Air Mikisew has ongoing negotiations with Suncor and Shell Canada to provide future charter and corporate shuttle services.

  With its growing success, MCFN has been able to provide its members with a return on their investment. More specifically, MCFN now defrays some of the costs of transport for its members. This includes two discounted seats and reduced rates on freight for MCFN passengers on each flight, awarded on a first-come, first-served basis. The point of the reduction is to ensure that MCFN members who invest as a band in the business venture also benefit from the airline initiative.

2 Population estimates were provided by membership clerks of the Mikisew Cree and Athabasca Chipewyan First Nations, the Métis Association of Fort Chipewyan, and by Improvement District Number 18 North.

3 Sources of Mikisew history include deCardinale 1996, Fumoleau 1976, McCormack 1984, and Selin 1999.

4 Examples of specific claims include a "breach of obligation arising from government administration of lands or assets, or illegal disposition of land. Non-compensation for reserve lands taken or damaged and fraud in connection with the disposition or acquisition of reserve lands by the federal government may also give rise to a specific claim" (Isaac 1999, 125).

Chapter 2: Neoliberalism Now

1 Because Canada is a federal state, the very concept of "the state" conflates the two levels of government, national and provincial. That their roles are separate is important to understand. At the same time, their goals overlap, since in recent years, provinces like Alberta and Ontario and the federal government have adopted a neoliberal stance, focusing on creating an economic climate conductive to investment by reducing their regulatory regimes. Hence, despite these independent roles, it is useful to draw on the notion of the state to encapsulate the way in which demands in the global economy transform the state-society relationship.

2 As of 2001, 58 percent of Aboriginal people lived on-reserve, or approximately 396,688 of a total population of 690,101 (DIAND 2003b, 5).

3 To elaborate, in 2002 the Cree signed the "Agreement Concerning a New Relationship between the Government of Quebec and the Crees of Quebec," also referred to as the "Paix de Braves." The agreement provides the Cree with an annual payment of $70 million over fifty years, indexed to the value of the output of hydroelectric, mining, and forestry industries in the territory, and a say in the development of future projects (Grand Council of the Crees 2007). Earlier, in 2000, the Aboriginal Pipeline Group (APG) was established to maximize the ownership of and benefits for Aboriginal people in the Mackenzie Valley natural gas pipeline. The main reason for creating the APG was to offer a new model for Aboriginal participation in the developing economy and to support greater independence and self-reliance among Aboriginal people. For more details see www.mvapg.com.

4 Additional causes of the recent shift in state goals are the increase in public concern over the social problems faced by First Nations people and the constitutional responsibility of both levels of government for First Nations people.

5 Since the failure of the proposed White Paper (DIAND 1969), in which the federal government proposed dismantling the Indian Act on the grounds that Indian problems were the consequence of special status, landmark legal cases have instead ultimately transformed the policy direction of the government. In the 1968 *Calder* case, the Nisga'a of northwestern British Columbia sought formal recognition of their Aboriginal title based on their occupation of the region since time immemorial. Although the case was lost due to a legal technicality (the application was dismissed on a procedural error), in its decision rendered in 1973 the court recognized the principle of Aboriginal title. Justice Emmett Hall went so far as to suggest that the Nisga'a still held occupancy-based title. The Trudeau government, already stung by its disastrous White Paper, announced shortly thereafter that it was prepared to negotiate outstanding land claims.

6 Green (1997, 60) argues that the "effective reassertion of First Nations jurisdiction spells limitations for federal and provincial governments, and for the corporate interests that those governments have served so well to date. It potentially means limited, terminated, or more costly access to natural resources, regulatory restrictions concerning environmental matters, community development and infrastructure, and required engagement with the primarily unskilled First Nations labour force."

7 This assessment is also supported by the 1985 Task Force to Review Comprehensive Claims Policy, which observed that the settlement of land claims has been achieved "only when the federal government was eager to facilitate an economic development project" (Wotherspoon and Satzewich 1993, 40).

8 Arguably, other forces drive First Nations policy, such as constitutional and legal obligations – s. 91 (24) and s. 35 of the Constitution Act – and international considerations/pressures.

9 According to the 2001 census, the national proportion of First Nations people with postsecondary credentials increased to 38 percent in 2001 from 33 percent in 1996. During the same year, 53.4 percent of all adult Canadians were university graduates (Statistics Canada 2006).

10 Previous models include the Native Economic Development Program (NEDP) of the 1970s and the Canadian Aboriginal Economic Development Strategy (CAEDS) of the 1980s.

11 It does not, however, impede the state's project of facilitating the accumulation of ever more concentrated wealth.

Chapter 3: Searching for Self-Determination

1 For more on Treaty 8, see Indian and Northern Affairs Canada, "Treaties – Historic Treaty Information," www.ainc-inac.gc.ca.
2 The Métis who lived in the settlement and who opted out of Treaty 8 were not afforded the same treatment as treaty Indians in the community. For instance, they had no promise of health care nor did they have reserve lands. In terms of education, there were no subsidies for Métis children. Yet, because of kinship ties and for economic reasons, the Métis, like the Cree and the Chipewyan, lived off the land, such that in the early days, it was difficult to determine their exact numbers. Thus, in spite of legal distinctions imposed by Treaty 8, there was considerable fluidity in band memberships, with persons and families "living the Indian mode of life" often added to treaty rolls. An important result of the treaty, therefore, was the division of local indigenous groups, which would facilitate federal government control over them.
3 Land was set aside according to the population count of 1972 (Brown 1978).
4 According to federal documents, MCFN lawyer Bob Young "reiterated that he is of the view the settlement with the Cree Band should be primarily between the federal government and the Band, and that the Province's role would be minimal. He was assuming that, if pushed, the Province would kill the deal and the Band would not achieve a settlement" (Zaharoff 1982a, 2).
5 It is important to remind the reader of the context in which these negotiations occurred. The 1974 OPEC crisis had led to a global concern over the price of oil and gas. Then, in 1981, the federal government introduced the National Energy Program (NEP), which outraged the province of Alberta. It was also during this time that tar sand production virtually came to a halt. After some time, the province of Alberta decided to negotiate on a bilateral basis with the federal government to repeal the NEP, which was particularly damaging to its economy.

Chapter 4: The Politics of Change

1 The Nisga'a Nation in the Naas Valley, British Columbia, pursued its comprehensive claim to traditional territories for over a century. The Nisga'a Final Agreement was initialled by representatives of the nation and the governments of Canada and British Columbia in August 1998 and ratified by all parties between November 1998 and April 2000. Similarly, the Sechelt Indian Band Self-Government Act came into force in October 1986. Approximately nine months later an accompanying piece of legislation, the Sechelt Indian Government District Enabling Act, was proclaimed by the province of British Columbia (see Cassidy and Bish 1989, 135). Other examples are the Nunavut Act and the Yukon Umbrella Agreement.
2 "Nunee" is a Dene word meaning "together." The formation of the health authority coincided with the decentralization of policy delivery in Alberta. This decentralization was an important part of the overall shift in health care because Alberta's regional authorities started overseeing delivery of social programs within the province. Nunee is unique because it is unofficially considered one of eighteen regional health authorities in the province of Alberta, even though it falls under federal jurisdiction.
3 Mikisew Cree First Nation operated Mistee Seepee Development Corporation Ltd. until April 1999, at which point it became Mikisew Technical Services (Palmer 1996, 1). The greatest housing need is for three-bedroom units. During 1996, 27 three-bedroom units, 15 two-to-three-bedroom units and 20 three-to-four-bedroom units were built. A one-bedroom unit (650 sq. ft) is $65,000. A two-bedroom unit (825 sq. ft) is $82,000 (ibid.).
4 As part of a governance initiative, one MCFN councillor is assigned the portfolio of education and sits on the board as one of the MCFN representatives.
5 Athabasca Delta Community School, Grades K-12: Number of professional staff – 19; Paraprofessionals – 11; Community Liaisons – 1; Assistant Councillor – 1; Students – 281. Special Programs: Special Education, Native Language, Home Economics, Industrial Arts, Drop-out Recovery, Youth Challenge Program.
6 In 2000, there was no Grade 12 graduation ceremony since no one qualified.

Chapter 5: The Economics of Change

1 For a more contemporary discussion, see Keith 2001.

2 The province of Alberta also became involved in the oil sands project when it was awarded control over resources in 1930. The provincial role, however, remained limited to matters pertaining to leasing of lands and royalties.

3 The Syncrude Project is a joint venture undertaking among Canadian Oil Sands Ltd. (36.74 percent), ConocoPhillips Oil Sand Partnership (9.03 percent), Imperial Oil Resources (25 percent), Mocal Energy Ltd. (5 percent), Murphy Oil Company Ltd. (5 percent), Nexen Oil Sands Partnership (7.23 percent), and Petro-Canada Oil and Gas (12 percent). See www. cos-trust.com/asset.

4 The person is referring specifically to the withdrawal of Atlantic Richfield Company in 1974.

5 The TLE funds awarded to MCFN at the time of the TLE settlement have been held in trust, locked into a capital account requiring the high approval rate of 75 percent of the voting membership for expenditure. Per capita distributions from the fund are strictly prohibited. Instead, interest is spent or invested at the discretion of the chief and council for the benefit of the entire membership.

6 The Super 8 has proven to be a very successful venture. The motel has been operating at 93 percent occupancy and was recipient of a very prestigious award in the hotel industry for the best managed and cleanest Super 8 in Canada (Mikisew Cree First Nation 2002d, 1).

7 In 1992, Gordon Benoit, a Treaty 8 Indian, commenced a court action claiming that Treaty 8 Indians were given an oral pledge in 1899, at the time of the signing of the treaty, that they and their descendants would be exempt from paying tax. In March 2002, the Federal Trial Court ruled in favour of Mr. Benoit, declaring that descendants of Treaty 8 Indians do not have to pay any tax at any time for any reason. In June 2003, the Federal Court of Appeal reversed the trial judgment, dismissing Mr. Benoit's claim. The Supreme Court of Canada's decision on 29 April 2004 not to hear the appeal means the Federal Court of Appeal judgment still stands (Mikisew Cree First Nation 2002c, 1; CBC 2002c). According to Bill Erasmus, vice chief of the Assembly of First Nations, First Nations governments are the only governments that properly have authority to tax First Nation members (CBC North 2003).

8 According to the INAC website, over eighty First Nations collect property tax, of which MCFN is one (DIAND 2004a).

9 The success of 2000 Plus has not been without obstacles. Despite their initial aim to work with the local First Nations communities to build companies that hire local people and provide important services, Syncrude officials still encountered hostility from the Chipewyan band in Fort Chipewyan. They noticed that 2000 Plus was focusing its hiring on the Cree band, and the Chipewyan weren't getting access to any opportunities. Acrimony between the two groups was resolved when Syncrude became more cognizant of how the community functioned and set out to assist the Chipewyan band in a similar way. The result was the creation of Denesuline, which employs seventy Chipewyan people and handles all the waste management on the Syncrude and Suncor sites. Reflecting on their oversight, Syncrude officials commented on how they had been so proud of 2000 Plus, because it had just started and taken off and had become a great company, that they hadn't been able to understand how they could be accused of not helping or supporting the community. This oversight led the company to focus on building business relationships with other First Nations in the region, such as the band at Fort MacKay, which lives in the shadow of Syncrude. By determining what the community needed, Syncrude has been more able to help and satisfy those needs. Yet Syncrude remains proud of its connection to the Cree band, pointing out how MCFN managed to "get on their feet" and become a highly advanced community, ahead of the other communities in the region, despite its isolation and remote northern location.

10 Focused on heavy equipment operations (excavation, grading, landscaping, ditching, packing, gravel hauling, raking, and brush/forest clearing), Neegan Development Corporation Ltd. is a versatile company with expertise in the heavy equipment and construction business. The corporation also offers services in project management and construction (i.e., surveying, safety consulting and training, water and vacuum truck services, and tree planting).

11 As one member explained, "We had a discussion. They had five or ten shares for sale. We sat and talked. We don't have the money" (Interview with MCFN member 2000i).
12 Rath speculates that the claim is worth $10 billion, which means it could ultimately bankrupt the province and, in the interim, unbalance the stable political environment that attracts energy companies to the region (Thomson 1999).

Chapter 6: Transforming First Nations Governance

1 The typical-disparity group was the largest of the three groups and showed a typical level of disparity in the four socioeconomic indicators relative to the average Canadian community. High-disparity groups were characterized by below-average conditions for all four variables.
2 The MCFN, ACFN, and Métis groups all have different status within the Fort Chipewyan community. Although membership in each group has always meant differences in social power, today, financial status adds yet another dimension of difference to these groups; membership within one collective is considered more advantageous than membership in another. MCFN is not only the biggest First Nation in the community but also the wealthiest, making it a "have" First Nation. ACFN is also a "have" band, though operating on a much smaller scale, leaving the Métis, by comparison, as the "have not" group within the community.
3 The notion of being a "have" group is not limited to First Nations groups but also to regions disproportionately inhabited by First Nations peoples within Canada. As the perception of increased independence is primarily associated with resource development activity, other First Nations and government leaders in Canada proclaim that it is just a matter of time before the Yukon, the Northwest Territories, and Nunavut will become "have" regions, much like Alberta, thanks to oil and gas exploration. Clearly, both individual First Nations and territories alike seek to become "have" groups through the economic benefits resource development brings.

References

Interviews

In the course of research, I conducted thirty-two interviews in spring 2000. All of them have been treated confidentially.

Interview with federal government representative. 2000a. 15 April. Fort Chipewyan, AB.
Interview with federal government representative 2000b. 15 April. Fort Chipewyan, AB.
Interview with federal government representative. 2000c. 29 May. Edmonton, AB.
Interview with federal government representative. 2000d. 6 June. Edmonton, AB.
Interview with provincial government representative. 2000a. 25 April. Fort Chipewyan, AB.
Interview with provincial government representative. 2000b. 11 May. Edmonton, AB.
Interview with provincial government representative. 2000c. 11 May. Edmonton, AB.
Interview with provincial government representative. 2000d. 5 May. Edmonton, AB.
Interview with MCFN member. 2000a. 13 April. Fort Chipewyan, AB.
Interview with MCFN member. 2000b. 14 April. Fort Chipewyan, AB.
Interview with MCFN member. 2000c. 14 April. Fort Chipewyan, AB.
Interview with MCFN member. 2000d. 14 April. Fort Chipewyan, AB.
Interview with MCFN member. 2000e. 14 April. Fort Chipewyan, AB.
Interview with MCFN member. 2000f. 16 April. Fort Chipewyan, AB.
Interview with MCFN member. 2000g. 17 April. Fort Chipewyan, AB.
Interview with MCFN member. 2000h. 17 April. Fort Chipewyan, AB.
Interview with MCFN member. 2000i. 17 April. Fort Chipewyan, AB.
Interview with MCFN member. 2000j. 18 April. Fort Chipewyan, AB.
Interview with MCFN member. 2000k. 18 April. Fort Chipewyan, AB.
Interview with MCFN member. 2000l. 25 April. Fort Chipewyan, AB.
Interview with MCFN member. 2000m. 25 April. Fort Chipewyan, AB.
Interview with MCFN member. 2000n. 25 April. Fort Chipewyan, AB.
Interview with MCFN member. 2000o. 25 April. Fort Chipewyan, AB.
Interview with MCFN member. 2000p. 26 April. Fort Chipewyan, AB.
Interview with MCFN member. 2000q. 27 May. Edmonton, AB.
Interview with MCFN member. 2000r. 5 June. Edmonton, AB.
Interview with MCFN member. 2000s. 5 June. Fort McMurray, AB.
Interview with Suncor representative. 2000. 5 May. Fort McMurray, AB.
Interview with Syncrude representative. 2000a. 5 May. Fort McMurray, AB.
Interview with Syncrude representative. 2000b. 5 May. Fort McMurray, AB.
Interview with Syncrude representative. 2000c. 5 May. Fort McMurray, AB.
Interview with Syncrude representative. 2000d. 5 May. Fort McMurray, AB.

Other Sources

Abele, Frances. 1987. "Canadian Contradictions: Forty Years of Northern Political Development." *Arctic* 40, 4:310-20.

—. 1997. "Understanding What Happened Here: The Political Economy of Indigenous Peoples." In *Understanding Canada: Building on the New Canadian Political Economy,* ed. Wallace Clement, 118-40. Montreal and Kingston: McGill-Queen's University Press.

Abele, Frances, Katherine A. Graham, and Allan Maslove. 1999. "Negotiating Canada: Changes in First Nations Policy over the Last Thirty Years." In *How Ottawa Spends: 1999-2000,* ed. Leslie Pal, 251-92. Don Mills, ON: Oxford University Press.

Aboriginal Pipeline Group. 2007. "Aboriginal Pipeline Group: Maximizing Economic Benefits through Ownership in a Northern Pipeline." 1 August. www.mvapg.com.

Adams, Stuart. 1998. *Fort Chipewyan: Way of Life Study: Summary Report.* Vancouver: Stuart Adams and Associates.

Albo, Gregory, and Jane Jenson. 1997. "Remapping Canada: The State in the Era of Globalization." In *Understanding Canada: Building on the New Canadian Political Economy,* ed. Wallace Clement, 215-39. Montreal and Kingston: McGill-Queen's University Press.

Anderson, F.J. 1986. *Natural Resources in Canada: Economic Theory and Policy.* Agincourt, ON: Methuen Publications.

Anderson, Robert B. 1997. "Corporate/Indigenous Partnerships in Economic Development: The First Nations in Canada." *World Development* 25, 9: 1483-1503.

Angus, Murray. 1990. *"And the Last Shall Be First": Native Policy in an Era of Cutbacks.* Ottawa: First Nations Rights Coalition (Project North).

Armstrong, Robin. 1999. *Rural and Small Town Canada Analysis Bulletin* 1, 8 (June).

Asch, Michael. 1977. "The Dene Economy." In *Dene Nation: The Colony Within,* ed. Mel Watkins, 47-61. Toronto: University of Toronto Press.

—. 1985. "Native Peoples." In *The New Practical Guide to Canadian Political Economy,* ed. Daniel Drache and Wallace Clement, 152-61. Toronto: James Lorimer and Company.

Bakker, Isabella, and Katherine Scott. 1997. "The Post-Liberal Keynesian Welfare State." In *Understanding Canada: Building on the New Canadian Political Economy,* ed. Wallace Clement, 286-310. Montreal and Kingston: McGill-Queen's University Press.

Barnsley, Paul. 2001. "Interim Overhaul of Indian Act Planned." *Windspeaker* 18, 10 (February): 1.

Black, Joan. 1999. "David Tuccaro: Creating Opportunities for Others Motivates Businessman." *Windspeaker* (1 April): 4. www.ammsa.com/achieve/AA99-D.Tuccaro.html.

Boldt, Menno. 1993. *Surviving as Indians: The Challenges of Self-Government.* Toronto: University of Toronto Press.

Brethour, Patrick. 2002. "Syncrude Owners Want It to Rein in Cost Overrun." *Globe and Mail,* 4 October, B3.

—. 2003. "Native Claims Target Oil Patch." *Globe and Mail,* 22 February, B5.

Brodie, Janine. 1995. *Politics on the Margins.* Halifax: Fernwood Publishing.

—. 1997a. "Meso-Discourses, State Forms and the Gendering of Liberal-Democratic Citizenship." *Citizenship Studies* 1, 2: 223-242.

—. 1997b. "The New Political Economy of Regions." In *Understanding Canada: Building on the New Political Economy,* ed. Wallace Clement, 240-61. Montreal and Kingston: McGill-Queen's University Press.

Brown, R.D. 1978. Letter to the Minister, Indian and Northern Affairs, Ottawa, 6 February.

Cairns, Alan. 2000. *Citizens Plus: First Nations People and the Canadian State.* Vancouver: UBC Press.

Campbell, Maria. 1973. *Halfbreed.* Toronto: McClelland and Stewart.

Canada. 1982. *Constitution Act, 1982.* Schedule B to the *Canada Act 1982* (U.K.), 1982, c. 11.

—. 1996. *Report of the Royal Commission on Aboriginal Peoples.* 5 vols. Ottawa: Canada Communication Group Publishing.

Cassidy, Frank. 1990. "First Nations Governments in Canada: An Emerging Field of Study." *Canadian Journal of Political Science* 23, 1 (March): 73-99.

Cassidy, Frank, and John Bish. 1989. *Indian Government: Its Meaning and Practice.* Lantzville, BC: Oolichan Books and the Institute for Research on Public Policy.

CBC. 2001. "Ottawa Backs Northern Development Plan." *CBC News,* 17 August. www.cbc.ca.

—. 2002a. "Canada Appealing Decision to Exempt Natives from Taxation." *CBC News,* 19 November. www.cbc.ca.

—. 2002b. "Cree Chiefs Endorse Resources Deal with Quebec." *CBC News,* 5 February. www. cbc.ca.

—. 2002c. "No Targets for Northern Hire, Says De Beers." *CBC News,* 6 December. www. cbc.ca.

—. 2002d. "Oil Sheikhs of the Prairies." *CBC News,* 19 December. www.cbc.ca.

CBC North. 2003. "Aboriginal Tax Dodge Questioned." *CBC North,* 9 April. www.cbc.ca.

Clement, Wallace, and Glen Williams. 1997. "Resources and Manufacturing in Canada's Political Economy." In *Understanding Canada: Building on the New Canadian Political Economy,* ed. Wallace Clement, 43-63. Montreal and Kingston: McGill-Queen's University Press.

Davidson, Gordon Charles. 1918. *The North West Company.* Berkeley: University of California Press.

DeBrou, Dave, and Bill Waiser, eds. 1992. *Documenting Canada: A History of Modern Canada in Documents.* Saskatoon, SK: Fifth House Publishers.

deCardinale, Joseph. 1996. *Fort Chipewyan: A Community Profile and Attitude and Perceptions, 1995-1996.* Fort Chipewyan: Mikisew Cree First Nation.

DeSantis, Solange. 2002. "Native Affairs." *Globe and Mail. Report on Business,* 31 May.

DIAND (Department of Indian Affairs and Northern Development). 1969. *Statement of the Government of Canada on Indian Policy* (The White Paper). Ottawa: Department of Indian Affairs and Northern Development.

—. 1996a. "Canada and Mikisew Cree First Nation Agree to Develop New Self-Government and Financial Arrangements." 18 November. www.ainc-inac.gc.ca.

—. 1996b. "Mikisew Cree First Nation: Backgrounder." November. www.ainc-inac.gc.ca.

—. 2001. "Communities First: First Nations Governance." News releases January-April 2001. 30 April. www.ainc-inac.gc.ca/nr/prs.

—. 2002a. "Communities First: First Nations Governance Consultation Report – Phase 1." http://www.ainc-inac.gc.ca/ps/lts/fng/prev/CRP1_J02_e.html.

—. 2002b. "New Economic Development Funds for First Nations Create Access to Oil and Gas Industry." News releases January-April 2002. 5 March. Hay River, NWT. www.ainc-inac.gc.ca/nr/prs.

—. 2003a. "Athabasca Tribal Council Inks Historic Oil Sands Deal." 4 February. www.ainc-inac.gc.ca/nr/ecd/ssd/otm22_e.html.

—. 2003b. *Basic Departmental Data, 2002.* First Nations and Northern Statistics Section. Ottawa: Ministry of Indian Affairs and Northern Development.

—. 2004a. *Appendix C: Property Tax Collecting First Nations.* Indian and Northern Affairs Canada. www.ainc-inac.gc.ca/pr/ra/bbt/apc_e.html.

—. 2004b. "Mikisew Slings & Safety Ltd., Quality Products, Guaranteed Services." *Grassroots: First Nation Business in Alberta* (Winter): 5. www.ainc-inac.gc.ca/ab/pubs/gr04a_e.html.

—. 2007. First Nation Profiles. sdiprod2.inac.gc.ca/FNProfiles/FNProfiles_home.htm.

Dickason, Olive Patricia. 1992. *Canada's First Nations: A History of Founding Peoples from Earliest Times.* Toronto: McClelland and Stewart.

Ellwood, Wayne. 2001. *The No-Nonsense Guide to Globalization.* Toronto: New Internationalist Publications and Between the Lines.

Fisher, A.D. 1981. "A Colonial Education System; Historical Changes and Schooling in Fort Chipewyan." *Canadian Journal of Anthropology* 2, 1: 37-44.

Fort Chipewyan Cree Band. 1982. *Principles and Proposals for Treaty 8 Entitlement Settlement.* Fort Chipewyan: Fort Chipewyan Cree Band.

Francoli, Paco. 2002. "Nault Says Ottawa Is Prepared to Help Build Northern Pipelines but Stresses Market Will Have Final Say." *The Hill Times,* 19 August. www.thehilltimes.ca.

Fumoleau, René. 1976. *As Long As This Land Shall Last: A History of Treaty 8 and Treaty 11 1870-1939.* Toronto: McClelland and Stewart.

Graham, Katherine. 1987. "Indian Policy and the Tories: Cleaning Up after the Buffalo Jump." In *How Ottawa Spends, 1987-88,* ed. M.J. Prince, 237-67. Toronto: Methuen.

Grand Council of the Crees. 2007. "Grand Chief Matthew Mukash's Remarks at Premier's Event at HydroQuebec, Montreal, 11 January. www.gcc.ca.

Green, Joyce A. 1997. "Exploring Identity and Citizenship: First Nations Women, Bill C-31 and the Sawridge Case." Ph.D. diss. University of Alberta.

—. 2001. "Canaries in the Mines of Citizenship: Indian Women in Canada." *Canadian Journal of Political Science* 34, 4: 715-38.

Green, Joyce, and Cora Voyageur. 1999. "Globalization and Development at the Bottom." In *Feminists Doing Development: A Practical Critique,* ed. Marilyn Porter and Ellen Judd, 142-57. London and New York: Zed Books.

Hawkes, David. 1985. *First Nations Self-Government: What Does It Mean?* Kingston, ON: Institute of Intergovernmental Relations.

—. 1989. *First Nations People and Government Responsibility: Exploring Federal and Provincial Roles.* Ottawa: Carleton University Press.

—. 2002. "Rebuidling the Relationship – The 'Made in Saskatchewan' Approach to First Nations Governance." Paper prepared for *Reconfiguring Aboriginal-State Relations, Canada: The State of the Federation, 2003.* 1-2 November, Institute of Intergovernmental Relations, Kingston, ON.

—, ed. 1995. *First Nations People and Government Responsibility.* Ottawa: Carleton University Press.

Hawthorn, H.B., ed. 1966. *Survey of the Contemporary Indians of Canada.* Ottawa: Department of Indian Affairs and Northern Development.

Hill, Roger, and Pamela Sloan. 1996a. "Canada: Native Peoples and Corporations." In *Native Americas,* 48-64. Ithaca, NY: Cornell University Press.

—. 1996b. "A New Era in Corporate Aboriginal Relations." *Canadian Business Review* (Spring): 22-25.

Hirsch, Joachim. 1997. "Globalization of Capital, Nation-States and Democracy." *Studies in Political Economy* 54:39-58.

Hoogvelt, Ankie. 1997. *Globalization and the Postcolonial World: The New Political Economy of Development.* Baltimore: John Hopkins University Press.

Humenuk-Bourke, Natalie. 2000. "Tele-health Enhancing Fort Chip: Research Project Focuses on Improving Health Service Delivery." *Fort McMurray Today,* 15 April, 3.

Hyndman, Lou. 1978. Letter to the Honourable Hugh Faulkner, Federal and Intergovernmental Affairs, Ottawa, 2 October.

Indian Claims Commission. 1998. *Indian Claims Commission Proceedings,* vol. 10. Ottawa: Minister of Public Works and Government Services Canada.

Innis, Harold A. 1927. *The Fur Trade in Canada.* Toronto: University of Toronto Press.

—. 1956a. *Essays in Canadian Economic History.* Toronto: University of Toronto Press.

—. 1956b. *The Fur Trade in Canada: An Introduction to Canadian Economic History.* 1930. Reprint, Toronto: University of Toronto Press.

Isaac, Thomas. 1991. "Authority, Rights and an Economic Base: The Reality of Self-Government." *Native Studies Review* 7, 2: 69-73.

—. 1999. *First Nations Law: Cases, Materials and Commentary.* 2nd ed. Saskatoon: Purich Publishing.

Kalt, Joseph P., and Stephen Cornell. 1992. "Reloading the Dice: Improving the Chances for Economic Development on American Indian Reservations." In *What Can Tribes Do? Strategies and Institutions in American Indian Economic Development,* ed. Joseph P. Kalt and Stephen Cornell, 1-59. Los Angeles: University of California.

Keith, Lloyd, ed. 2001. *North of Athabasca: Slave Lake and Mackenzie River Documents of the North West Company, 1800-1821.* Montreal and Kingston: McGill-Queen's University Press.

Keynes, John Maynard. 1936. *The General Theory of Employment, Interest and Money.* London: Macmillan.

Klak, Thomas, ed. 1998. *Globalization and Neoliberalism: The Caribbean Context.* Lanham, MD: Rowman and Littlefield.

Leake, Sophie. 1995. "First Nations Land Claims Discussed at SFU Forum." *The Peak* 91, 4 (25 September).

Macdonald, Mark. 2000. "Relearning our ABC's? The New Governance of First Nations

Economic Development in Canada." In *How Ottawa Spends 2000-2001,* ed. Leslie A. Pal, 161-84. Don Mills, ON: Oxford University Press.

McConnell, Richard G. 1893. "Report – District of Athabasca." Library and Archives Canada. www.collectionscanada.ca/treaty8/4_0_why_e/05130407_e.html.

McCormack, Patricia. 1984. "How the (North) West Was Won." Ph.D. diss., University of Alberta.

Mercredi, Ovide. 1994. "A Conversation with National Chief Ovide Mercredi." *Mawioni Journal* (Winter): 7.

Mercredi, Trish. 2002. "RE: Nunee inquiry." E-mail to.author, 30 April.

Mikisew Cree First Nation. 1995. *Mikisew Cree First Nation: Profile.* Fort McMurray: Printing Unlimited.

—. 1996. *Building First Nation Independence.* Fort Chipewyan: Mikisew Cree First Nation.

—. 1998. "Socio-Economic and Cumulative Impacts Assessment Statement on the Muskeg River Mine Project." March. Report prepared for Shell Canada.

—. 1999. Mikisew Cree First Nation. www.mikisew.org/index.html.

—. 2002a. "From the Desk of the CEO." *The Call of the Eagle* 1, 2 (March-April): 13.

—. 2002b. "MCFN Industry Relations Agreement." *The Call of the Eagle* 1, 2 (March-April): n.p.

—. 2002c. "Stunning Victory for Treaty 8 in Benoit Case." *The Call of the Eagle* 1, 2 (March-April): n.p.

—. 2002d. "Super 8 Motel." *The Call of the Eagle* 1, 2 (March-April): 13.

Mikisew Energy Services Group. 2007. Corporate profile. www.mesg.ca.

Monture-Angus, Patricia. 2001. Discussion: Alan Cairns, Patricia Monture-Angus, and Kathy Brock. *Bridging the Divide between First Nations People and the Canadian State,* 18-20. June. Montreal: Centre for Research and Information on Canada.

Moscovitch, Allan, and Andrew Webster. 1995. "Aboriginal Social Assistance Expenditures." In *How Ottawa Spends: 1995-1996,* ed. Susan Phillips, 209-35. Ottawa: Carleton University Press.

National Aboriginal Achievement Foundation. 1999. "National Aboriginal Achievement Awards." Past recipients: David Gabriel Tuccaro, Business and Commerce, 1999. www.naaf.ca.

Nguyen, Lily. 2003a. "Don't Blame Gas Prices on Oil Patch: EnCana Chief." *Globe and Mail,* 21 February, B5.

—. 2003b. "TCPL, Pipeline Group Strike Tentative Financing Agreement." *Globe and Mail,* 21 February, B1.

Notzke, Claudia. 1994. *First Nations People and Natural Resources in Canada.* North York: Captus Press.

Palmer, Max. 1996. "On Reserve Remote Housing Program." Mikisew Technical Services report, 23 July, Fort Chipewyan, AB.

Panitch, Leo. 1977. "The Role and Nature of the Canadian State." In *The Canadian State: Political Economy and Political Power,* ed. Leo Panitch, 3-27. Toronto: University of Toronto Press.

Park, Gary. 2006. "Dealing with the Deh Cho: Canada Tables Offer to End Mac Conflict." *Petroleum News* 11 (24): 1. www.petroleumnews.com.

Pearson, David. 1994. "Self-Determination and Indigenous Peoples in Comparative Perspective: Problems and Possibilities." *Pacific Viewpoint* 35, 2: 129-41.

Penashue, Peter. 2002. "Why I Made Peace with Bay Street." *Globe and Mail,* 3 December, A23.

Pitts, Gordon. 2002. "First Nations Law Firm Looks to the Future." *Globe and Mail,* 2 December, B10.

Plumptre, Tim, and John Graham. 1999. *Governance and Good Governance: International and First Nations Perspectives.* Ottawa: Institute on Governance.

Pratt, Larry. 1976. *The Tar Sands: Syncrude and the Politics of Oil.* Edmonton: Hurtig Publishers.

Prentice, P.E. James. 1998. *Athabasca Chipewyan First Nation Inquiry: Report on the W.A.C. Bennett Dam and Damage to Indian Reserve 201 Claim.* Ottawa: Indian Claims Commission.

Prince, Michael J., and Frances Abele. 2002. "Paying for Self-Determination: First Nations People, Self-Government and Fiscal Relations in Canada." Paper prepared for *Reconfiguring*

Aboriginal-State Relations, Canada: The State of the Federation, 1-2 November 2003, Institute of Intergovernmental Relations, Kingston, ON.

Regional Municipality of Wood Buffalo. 2006. Municipal Census 2006, Fort McMurray, AB. www.woodbuffalo.ab.ca.

Rozon, Gina. 2001. "Education for Self-Determination." *American Review of Canadian Studies* 31, 1-2: 61.

Salter, Liora, and Rick Salter. 1997. "Displacing the Welfare State." In *Understanding Canada: Building on the New Canadian Political Economy,* ed. Wallace Clement. Montreal and Kingston: McGill-Queen's University Press.

Saskatchewan Indian and Métis Affairs Secretariat.1994. *First Nations Policy Framework: Toward a Shared Destiny.* Saskatoon: Saskatchewan Indian and Métis Affairs Secretariat.

Selin, Ron. 1999. *Into the New Millennium, Our Story: The Mikisew Cree First Nation.* Edmonton: Western Communications.

Slowey, Gabrielle A. 2001. "Globalization and Self-Government: Impacts and Implications For First Nations in Canada." *American Review of Canadian Studies* 31, 1-2: 265-81.

Smith, Linda Tuhiwai. 1999. *Decolonizing Methodologies: Research and Indigenous Peoples.* New York: Zed Books.

Smith, Steve, and John Baylis, eds. 1997. *The Globalization of World Politics.* Oxford: Oxford University Press.

Statistics Canada. 2006. *2001 Census.* www12.statcan.ca/english/census01/home/index.cfm.

Syncrude Canada. 1997. *First Nations Review 1997.* Fort McMurray, AB: Syncrude Canada.

Taft, Kevin. 1997. *Shredding the Public Interest: Ralph Klein and 25 Years of One-Party Government.* Edmonton: University of Alberta Press and the Parkland Institute.

Thomson, Graham. 1999. "Lawyer Warns Suit Not 'Frivolous.'" *Edmonton Journal,* 24 June. www.edmontonjournal.com.

Tough, Frank. 1996. *"As Their Natural Resources Fail": Native Peoples and the Economic History of Northern Manitoba, 1870-1930.* Vancouver: UBC Press.

Vermillion, Roy B. 1991. "Understanding Our Past to Plan for the Future: A Case Study of Cree Education in Fort Chipewyan." MA thesis, University of British Columbia.

Waquan, Archie. 1992. *Presentation by the Mikisew Cree First Nation to the Royal Commission on Aboriginal Peoples.* 18 June. Fort Chipewyan, AB.

—. 1996. "Message from the Chief." In *Mikisew Cree First Nation: A Profile.* Fort McMurray: Printing Unlimited.

Watkins, Mel. 1977. "From Underdevelopment to Development." In *Dene Nation: The Colony Within,* ed. Mel Watkins, 84-99. Toronto: University of Toronto Press.

Weaver, Sally M. 1990. "A New Paradigm in Canadian Indian Policy for the 1990s." *Canadian Ethnic Studies* 22, 3: 8-17.

—. 1992. "Indian Government: A Concept in Need of a Definition." In *Pathways to Self-Determination,* ed. Leroy Little Bear, Menno Boldt, and J. Anthony Long, 65-68. Toronto: University of Toronto Press.

Williams, Allan. 1991. "New Transfer Payment Mechanisms." *CMA Magazine,* June.

Wittchen, Tara Lee. 2004. "Mikisew Energy Services Group Company Branching Out, Growing." Indian and Northern Affairs Canada. www.ainc-inac.gc.ca/nr/nwltr/bae/as022_e.html.

Wonders, William C. 1971. *Canada's Changing North.* Toronto: McClelland and Stewart.

Woods Gordon Management Consultants. 1981. *Cree Band – Ft. Chipewyan: Initial Assessment of Economic Prospects. Final Report.* Edmonton, AB: Woods Gordon Management Consultants.

Working Group on First Nations Participation in the Economy. 2001. "Strengthening First Nations Participation in the Economy." Report of the Working Group on First Nations Participation in the Economy to Federal-Provincial/Territorial Ministers Responsible for First Nations Affairs and National First Nations Leaders. 11 May.

Wotherspoon, Terry, and Vic Satzewich. 1993. *First Nations: Race, Class and Gender Relations.* Scarborough, ON: Nelson Canada.

Young, Robert. 1974. "Cree Band at Fort Chipewyan – Land Entitlement." Letter to Department of Indian and Northern Affairs, 28 August, Calgary.

Youngblood Henderson, James [sakej]. 1994. "Empowering Treaty Federalism" *Saskatchewan Law Review* 58:241-328.

Zaharoff, W.J. 1982a. "Cree-Chip Settlement Proposal Meetings May 6 and 7, 1982," Note to File: May 27. Ottawa: Indian and Northern Affairs Canada.

—. 1982b. "Cree-Chip Treaty Entitlement: Negotiating with Band October 12, 1982." Note to File: October 15. Ottawa: Indian and Northern Affairs Canada.

Index

Doghead, 3, 10, 36
Peace Point, 10
population on, 12, 80n2
in Saskatchewan TLE agreement, 76-77
residential schools, 70
revenue. *See* finances
Rhodes, Cecil, 24
Royal Commission on Aboriginal Peoples
(RCAP), 47, 74
royal commissions, xiii

Saskatchewan, 21, 76
Saskatchewan Treaty Land Entitlement
Framework Agreement, 76-77
schools. *See* education
Sechelt Indian Band Self-Government Act,
82n1
Sechelt Indian Government District
Enabling Act, 82n1
self-determination
definition of, 11-13, 18, 53-54
dilemmas of, 53, 78
economic dimension of, 11, 12, 19-23,
36-37, 63 (*see also* finances)
geography and, 77-78
history of, xiii
land and, 12
natural resources and, 12-13
neoliberal globalization and, xiv-xv, 10-
14, 17-18, 23, 73
off-reserve, 12-13
policy making and, 42
political dimension of, xv, 17-19 (*see
also* governance)
taxation and, 66
Treaty Land Entitlement and, 10
self-government, 7
self-sufficiency
as citizenship, 17-18
investment and, 13
natural resources and, 12-13
See also self-determination
Shell Canada, 80n1
Slave River, 56
Snap Lake, 78
Social Enhancement, 70-73
social problems, xiv, 70-73
neoliberalism and, 75
social programs, 18, 19, 28
funding of, 38-39
neoliberalism and, 53
transfer of, xv
*Statement of the Government of Canada on
Indian Policy* (1969), 33
state retrenchment, 32, 79
Stewart, Jack (Jock), 30-31

Stringham, Greg, 62
suicide, xiv, 44
Suncor, 58, 67, 69, 78
Super 8 Motel, 65, 83n6
sustainable economic development, 19-20
Syncrude, 78, 83n9
Cree people and, 59-73
education requirements of, 52
history of, 58, 59
influence of, 41-42
social reform and, 72
Syncrude Project, 83n3

tar sands, 6-7, 25-26, 33, 34
Cree people and, 62-73
employment in, 60
history of, 58, 59
MCFN suit for control of, 69
participation in, 37-38
revenue from, 35
size and wealth of, 62-63
See also oil and gas industry; Suncor;
Syncrude
Task Force to Review Comprehensive
Claims Policy, 81n7
taxation, 66, 83n7, 83n8
TecKnowledge Healthcare Systems, 44
Telehealth Research Project, 44-45
Tele-Visitations, 45
Third National Policy (TNP), 31
TLE. *See* Treaty Land Entitlement (TLE)
transcontinental railway, 25
treaties
in Canada, 9
with Cree, 26
Treaty 8, 7-10, 26, 27, 31, 69
Treaty Land Entitlement (TLE), 8-10, 54
capital base from, 76-77
definition of, 10
economic development after, 64-67
of Mikisew Cree, 33-35
restructuring after, 41-42
in Saskatchewan, 76
settlement from, 33-37, 83n5
tar sands project and, 63-64
Tuccaro, David, 67-68
Tuccaro, 68
2000 Plus Limited Partnership, 42, 67,
83n9

unemployment, xiv, 59

vision, xv
vision care, 44, 46

Waquan, Chief, 33, 40, 42, 47, 64

wards of the state, 16, 18, 74
water, xiv, 61
Watkins, Mel, 77
welfare state, xiv, 7-8, 16, 18, 27-28, 31
  as colonialism, 61
White Paper, 33, 81n5
Wood Buffalo National Park, 3-5, 7, 10,
  29, 33, 36, 57
Woodland Cree, 3-4, 7-8, 56
  See also Cree people

Young, Bob, 82n4
Yukon, 26
Yukon Umbrella Agreement, 82n1